RAPE – My Story

'Rape is totally and utterly destructive, striking right at the roots of a person's sense of self and worth. I would not have believed that the events of one hour on 6 March 1986 could have such devastating effects.'

Jill Saward
with Wendy Green

RAPE
My Story

Pan Books
London, Sydney and Auckland

First published in Great Britain 1990 by
Bloomsbury Publishing

This edition published 1991 by
Pan Books Ltd, Cavaye Place, London SW10 9PG

1 3 5 7 9 8 6 4 2

© Jill Saward and Wendy Green 1990

'Bread of Life' by Garth Hewitt © Word Music 1984

ISBN 0 330 31951 5

Printed in England by Clays Ltd, St Ives plc

by the
Grace of God
go I

CHAPTER ONE

Twelve strokes of the clock. Midnight. It is New Year's Day 1986. The past year has not been one of the best. I know what my prayer for this new one will be:

'Lord, give me a better year.'

I don't think I can cope with another like the last. There was so much hassle at work over the past six months. The boss and I just didn't see eye to eye. We were always having run-ins over such things as job descriptions, unions, and my training. Eventually he suggested that my twenty-first birthday in the middle of January would be a good time to start afresh. Somewhere else. I opted for Christmas Eve. If I had to go I didn't see why I should stay around to make sure Christmas and the New Year were covered by staff. Dad isn't the only one who can stick up for himself when necessary.

It doesn't bother me too much now when he is thought of as controversial, but I don't like him being branded 'the sex book vicar' because of a book he had published when I was ten. It was intended to counterbalance some of the permissive attitudes of the time, though no one would have thought so once the popular press got hold of the story. I couldn't understand why there was such a fuss. I was more concerned about how long it would be before Mum let me go down to the shops by myself than whether or not people should go to bed together before getting married.

Having a father who is a vicar was enough of a problem. When we lived in Beckenham, Dad had a 'real' job. He was Radio and Television Officer for the Church Information Office. We lived in a house that was ours and we had neighbours, unlike most of the vicarages we've lived in. I usually liked the houses but they were never the norm for the area. Some people were scared of going to them, and others, like tramps, came frequently. Not that Dad seemed to mind. He's a good communicator and administrator and can take most things in his stride. Prebendary of St Paul's Cathedral. Vicar of Ealing. Church Commissioner. Member of the General Synod. Hymn writer.

Helping to edit the new hymn book was another thing that landed him in hot water. It has updated versions of some of the hymns, including the National Anthem. Which didn't go down too well in some quarters. I was glad I was in Wales when that story broke, even though I knew Dad wasn't responsible for changing the words. I like singing some of his hymns, especially 'Baptised in Water' and 'Lord of the Cross of Shame', but I resented the hymn book taking up so much of his time over ten years. It's certainly not easy having such a well-known figure for a father, particularly when people seem to expect me to know everything he has done. He's always worked too hard, so there's never been a lot of time left over for the family.

I'm not keen on admitting it but I guess I must get my rebellious streak from Dad. Or his maternal grandfather. He was still alive when my sister and I were born, though he died later that year. He was Captain of the SS *Montrose*, on which the notorious Dr Crippen tried to escape to Canada after murdering his wife. Great-granddad had been following the case in the English papers and suspected that one of the passengers could be Crippen. He invited him to dine at his table to check further, and then alerted the police in the first radio message from sea to shore to be used in the detection of a crime.

Great-granddad had an eventful life, which included being

shipwrecked and trekking a hundred miles across Australia to escape someone intent on murdering him. When he died he was reliving the nightmare of a shipwreck. He would never talk about the worst one. He was Captain of the *Empress of Ireland*, the ship that lost the greatest number of passenger lives in peacetime. A Norwegian ship ploughed into them in the fog, and his ship went down in a matter of minutes. Over eight hundred passengers were drowned. He always thought he should have died too, but he lived till he was ninety-one.

My grandparents on Mum's side were pretty distinguished as well. My grandfather was a colonel and the author of several books, and my grandmother had an MBE for getting people out of a glass-roofed building during an air raid in the War. Grandpa was a lot older than Grandma. He died when my mum was about thirteen or fourteen. When Grandma retired she moved to Frinton on the east coast and we would often go down to stay with her during the holidays.

She died when I was ten. My twin sister cried, but I didn't. I mourned her six years later. It was Christmastime. Suddenly I missed Grandma and wished she had been alive for longer. It was just before a party and a friend who called wanted to know why I was upset. I felt such an idiot having to explain that I was crying about someone who had died six years before. It was weird. We didn't know Grandma all that well anyway. I think if I had known her longer I might not have missed her so much. She was a bit strict. She wasn't very happy that Mum was marrying a clergyman. Or that she worked part time stacking shelves in Sainsbury's, having trained as an English teacher.

Mum doesn't do things simply to please other people. She certainly doesn't go a bomb on the traditional role of vicar's wife. When we were younger she needed a job to pay my brother's school fees so she started working at Sainsbury's and has stayed with them for many years. She's very practical. She's seen lots of life through working seven or eight years in Chelsea, where she's

3

met everything from punks to Chelsea Pensioners. She wasn't too impressed when I became a cleaner at the YMCA, though. In fact, I enjoyed it more than most other jobs I'd done, apart from the problems with the boss. I got on well with the other cleaners. I like people who enjoy life and are upfront.

I remember a girl at grammar school asking me if I liked her new dress. When I said I didn't she gave me a lecture all the way home about being tactful. Some people don't like it when I give a straight answer to their question, but if they don't like the way I answer they shouldn't ask my opinions in the first place.

Pete understood, but he isn't here any more. He died of cancer three years ago. I was eating a burger at McDonald's when I was told and I've never been able to face them since. I only knew Pete for a few months but he became like a dad to me. He talked to me and gave me time and advice. He was the leader when I first came to work on the holiday mission here in North Wales, and he made me feel I had real potential and worth. He told me not to go with the crowd, but to do what I thought was right.

Maybe that's why I'm feeling a bit tearful. New Year has always been a special time to remember him and his family. At the same time, ever since I was fourteen Wales has been a place to go on my own, to cry away the built-up tension and prepare myself for the next onslaught. It's so nice to get away from home and family and all the people who know me; to be what I want to be, to let the emotions come out. I think if people have certain expectations of the vicar's daughter they have probably been disappointed. But that doesn't bother me. I don't think that being on display all the time has given me too many inhibitions, although I don't like living close to the church. I think the need for freedom is more to do with being a twin.

Pug and I are identical, but she has a mole on her left cheek. People frequently confuse us and I can't say I blame them. Occasionally, as I've got older, I will be in a shop and see myself in a mirror and think it's Pug. When we were little we were often taken for boys because we had short hair and didn't wear pretty-pretty clothes. Mum wasn't really a pretty-dress kind of person. She's very straightforward and down-to-earth. If she had the choice she'd wear trousers. So we used to wear trousers and T-shirts, and people just used to think 'boys'. When Mum was expecting us she would have liked another boy, but she also wanted twins, so we weren't too much of a disappointment. Her family seem to have trouble carrying boys. Joe's the only one in our family, and as we have an older sister he's outnumbered three to one.

Pug's not my twin's real name. I just started calling her that when we were about ten years old. I thought it was original and much better than her proper names. She has three and I don't like any of them. I don't think much of mine either. None of them are original to me. I made up the name Pug. I didn't know about pug dogs or people being pugnacious. All those things came out later. She was quite impressed to think there were dogs named after her. She quite likes them. I can't think why, they're the most revolting-looking animals. In return she called me Llij, which later turned into Snij. Before that, she lengthened it to illegitimate. I'd tease 'If I'm illegitimate, you are as well', but she reckoned Mum and Dad got married in the forty-five minutes between us. It was no use arguing. It was much easier to let her have her way.

When we were little I would rely on Pug quite a lot. I would let her make the friends. I wasn't very good with girls. I always preferred boys. They were more exciting. For years I wanted to be a boy. I hated dresses and girl-type activities and games. Playing cowboys and Indians with my brother was much more fun. He'd tie up our hands, and we'd have to get out. It was a great game.

Yet I enjoyed my early childhood – apart from being bullied for being twins and posh and intelligent. I don't think Mum and Dad ever took it seriously but at junior school we were bullied quite a lot. I would never hit the particular girl who was the worst. I just tried to talk to her, but that seemed to annoy her even more. Then, on the way home from school, the girls from the local comprehensive used to set on us because we lived in a big house.

We never seemed to get our act together somehow. There was always a sense that we weren't quite right in other people's eyes. When we went to grammar school the girls there thought of us as being fairly common people. One girl never spoke to me without being patronising or rude until the day before I left school and somebody told her we'd both got the same grade in English. It was the first time she actually spoke to me as if I were a human being. She was ultra-intelligent. Into Solzhenitsyn at eleven, that kind of thing.

We moved to Ealing when I was thirteen and I used to spend quite a lot of time in my fantasy world. I'd walk round the bricks in the garden, balancing, because they'd never been cemented in, creating a kind of soap opera a bit like *Brookside* in my mind. Very down-to-earth, nothing spectacular. I'm sure somebody in my imaginary family was called Laura. It was funny when I found out Pug did it too. I suppose it was our escape route, a way of establishing our own identities. We were living through other people, but they were special to us and nobody else knew about them. They got married, had kids, just day-to-day normal events. The kind of life I thought I'd be living one day, no longer feeling rather lonely and cut off.

I don't think it was because we only saw my Dad on rare occasions. We were used to that situation most of the time. We saw Mum a lot more. I think it was just the inability to maintain friendships. I never made friends with women very well. Pug was far more into making friends with girls. I would be a bit of a leech on those friendships. I always thought it was sad we didn't have a special friend but I don't suppose one would have lasted. I thought girls were boring. Maintaining relationships with females has never been my strongest point. I think it's easier with men. They can cope with picking up where you left off a lot easier. Women want a more constant relationship.

Pug and I have never admitted to being close, but we are. Fairly. She's probably not as much of a realist as I am. She likes things to be nice and to have happy endings. I'm probably not so idealistic. It's difficult to work out. Where I'd say we were different somebody else might say we're exactly the same. My dad once described us as 'Starstruck and Butch', after the television cops, Starsky and Hutch. I wasn't particularly impressed but it's a fair representation. Dad gave the illustration that if we both had heavy suitcases to get to a station Pug would stand and flutter her eyelashes, and somebody would rush to her aid, whilst I'd just get on and do the job myself. I'm not afraid to get my hands dirty. I wouldn't say Pug is afraid, but she'd rather somebody else did the work.

When we were teenagers she always seemed to have boyfriends, although I'm not sure how old she was when she first started going out with someone. We didn't talk about boys. We didn't really like the same types. My taste in men inclined towards the tall, dark and handsome. Pug liked blonds. She became engaged last year and I'm still not used to the idea. It seems strange to think she could be married before me, even if she did have a head start in the dating stakes.

I had my first kiss when I was fourteen. The boy was three years older. He was the person who told me most about the facts of life. I didn't have a proper boyfriend till I was seventeen. That lasted six whole weeks but we rarely saw each other as we were both busy. There wasn't anyone else for a couple more years. Then that one lasted all of six weeks, too. I've liked a lot of people since, but didn't go out with anyone till David, my current boyfriend, came along.

I met him at the YMCA, but I don't think that went down too well. Staff aren't meant to form relationships with residents. David is a security guard so he used to be around a lot in the mornings, after he had finished his 'day' and was on his way to bed. I found him attractive but we didn't really get to know each other until the room he shared was found to be full of mould and condensation. It was checked by an architect and found to be way above legal limits. The men had to be moved, so I helped David carry some of his stuff and we got talking. He asked me out and I accepted. I don't really agree with going out with non-Christians but he seems open to listening.

Ah well, it's early days yet. Anything could happen. David has spent Christmas at home in Scotland, and I am in Wales for the New Year. Our time of prayer is over. I must collect my wandering thoughts. We are going down to the beach for the usual first service of the year. It's been snowing and even the beach is covered. That should be interesting. Singing in the snow. We mustn't forget the champagne. I bought some earlier so we could celebrate the New Year in style. It's going to be a good one. I have given up that nightmare of a job; I will be twenty-one in two weeks' time; and when I get home David will be back in London, waiting for me. There's no knowing what's in store in the months that lie ahead, but I'm not particularly bothered. I'm tired, looking forward to a rest, and know God is in control. That is sufficient.

CHAPTER TWO

By the grey March light filtering through the window I know
I should be on the move. Instead I snuggle further under my
duvet. It's far too cosy to get up. The new terry stretch sheet I
bought recently makes quite a difference. What day is it anyway?
Wednesday? Thursday? Who cares. When you have no job, no
routine, all the days roll into one. The first time I was unemployed I quite liked it. I used to watch a lot of TV. Then, after
the initial period, it began to get boring. This time it is even
worse. I get very frustrated. Not that I've sat on my backside
for the whole of January and February, far from it.

David's job with the security firm didn't last long after I left
the YMCA. He packed it in soon after Christmas and took a
job labouring on a building site. While he was looking round
for work he found me a temporary job at a private school. I've
trained as a nursery nurse, so the job looked promising. I was
to work with children from two and a half to five years old.
No problem. Until I discovered the teaching methods being
used. Everything seemed to be learned parrot-fashion, and there
was little scope for imagination. To make matters worse, I
picked up a bad cough and cold. When my three-week stint
was up I was more than happy to leave.

Now I am back to square one, only more so: no job, and a
wretched cough that kept me awake half the night, even when
I tried sleeping on my beanbag. The pain in my ribs is terrible.

It seems to have started last weekend while we were in Scotland with David's family for a short break. I wasn't feeling too well before we went but I thought the fresh air might do me good. Some hope. To make matters worse I've got another bout of thrush.

I feel badly in need of sympathy but there is no one to take pity on me. Mum and Pug are at work. Dad is in his study working. Rachel got married when Pug and I were seventeen. She wanted us to be her bridesmaids but I thought we would look silly. I don't like to see twins dressed alike. It makes them lose their identity. Besides, I didn't really want Rachel to leave home. She lost lots of weight for her wedding and wasn't cuddly any more. She still comes back fairly regularly, but it isn't the same.

Sometimes I wonder what it will be like when Pug leaves. Not that it will be for a while yet, knowing the way Pug's mind works. The romanticist. Everything will have to be just right at her wedding. It's strange to think we should both be going out with men called Dave, although her David is a couple of years older than us. Mine's four months younger, much to my embarrassment.

One good thing, at least Joe will have to come home for Pug's wedding. These days it's hard to keep track of him. Being a journalist he's hardly ever around. I suppose I ought to be used to it. He was never at home during termtime when we were younger. As the son and heir he was packed off to boarding school from the age of ten.

None of us liked the fact that he was getting private education but we just had to accept it. He's had lots of problems with his schooling because we'd moved around so much when he was little. I think at one stage he went to three schools in a year. I know Mum resented having to buy a different uniform each time. The private schooling paid off in the end, though. He's got O levels, A levels, S levels and a degree. Pug and I just make do with O levels. Joe's still special. I missed him a lot when he went away to school and I still do. It's nice having a big brother, even if he wasn't all that thrilled about getting twin sisters.

That's better. I nearly managed a smile there. It's time to sit up and snap out of it. Feeling sorry for myself never did me much good. Think of Mrs Richmond. How often do I hear her complain? She's a Lancashire lass, who lives in a local sheltered housing complex. Her husband died about twenty years ago, but she always looks on the bright side of life. She's a real inspiration to me. I won't say she never says a rude word about anyone because she can be quite naughty at times about her companions, but some of them do go on, and she doesn't get many callers from the outside world. A visit from our young people's group once a month is the high spot of her social calendar. She doesn't seem to let it get her down, though; she's always laughing and cracking jokes. I went to visit her on my birthday and I can't think of a better way to have spent the time. She's just like a granny. I hope I can be like that at her age. It wouldn't do me any harm if I had half her zest for living now, come to think of it. I wonder what she would give to be twenty-one again? Pug and I certainly haven't done too badly out of it. Pug made her eighteenth birthday the official one, but I decided to wait till my twenty-first. We didn't intend to make people dig into their pockets twice, but they seemed a bit embarrassed to skimp by giving a present to just one of us.

The day before our twenty-first we went out for a meal in a posh restaurant in Clapham. It was into nouvelle cuisine, but Pug and I were not impressed. I had five bits of lamb arranged as a flower with a bean as a stalk and a few vegetables. Later Mum bought us a pizza, which was far cheaper, more enjoyable and much more filling.

Being a bit short of cash doesn't really worry me, even on unemployment benefit. It's still more than I've ever had before. I've never resented the fact we didn't have lots to spend, even if a bit of extra pocket money might have come in useful at times.

When I was at school I occasionally talked about getting a Saturday job, but Mum said I'd be too tired and needed to concentrate on schoolwork. From the time I was sixteen I used to sleep a lot. I found being a teenager hard. I was quite lonely, didn't make friends easily, and was often misunderstood.

Maybe having a twin sister was enough. Even so, there came a time when Pug and I needed to do our own thing. We divided our room in Fulham and have our own rooms now in Ealing. My room is entirely my domain. It's painted white with a big blue star shape on the wall, which has my name in the middle, in case anyone should have any doubts that it's my territory.

There's a built-in cupboard and sink along one wall, a bookcase and music box next to my bed, and a chest of drawers in the far corner. The trolley containing my display of pigs is next to that. I'm very fond of my pig collection. I started it when I was about ten. I thought pigs were lovely creatures who had had a bit of a raw deal as far as animals went. One of my first pigs was Wilbur. He came from my grandma's when she died. Now I have over sixty, in pottery, china, plastic, wax and glass. You name it, I've got it.

My soft toys sit on the floor, apart from Scrubby, who has moved into Rachel's room because he's the same colour as the furniture in there. Scrubby's one of my favourites. I got him the first or second time I went to see a play at Wormwood Scrubs. A woman at church who worked with the WRVS took me. She used to serve tea and coffee in the prison canteen, where the prison visitors and wives went, and she would get tickets for the plays done by the 'lifers'.

It was weird going inside on my first visit. The massive gates of the Scrubs clanged behind me, and I knew I couldn't get out. There were more gates, a perimeter fence, barbed wire, razor wire, guards walking around, and Alsatians which looked fierce enough to kill. We went on through the buildings, past A, B and D wings, with the prisoners hurling abuse and suggestive remarks from the cells. I could see the bread and the rubbish they'd thrown out in a pile below their windows. Further along they had their own little budgie aviary and garden to look after.

Eventually we walked into the recreation room of D wing, where there were prisoners on the door to welcome us and show us to our seats. I couldn't help thinking, 'These blokes are murderers and rapists', although the one thing we didn't do was ask why they were in there. During the interval they sold Christmas cards and hot drinks. I tried once to get a drink of water because I don't drink tea or coffee, but they only had the facilities for hot water, and they couldn't get out to fetch a cup of cold water. They were always collecting money, persuading it out of people for raffles and charities, children's charities normally. Once they released a single and we were able to buy one. They had a bloke who was a very good artist and they sold his paintings. Then there were the soft toys made by the prisoners, often for local children. I suppose it's a way of passing the time. It's obvious they want to do a good job and put love and care into what they do. Scrubby is actually mine *and* Pug's, but she hasn't had a look in yet. Monkey came from there too. I ordered a hippo, but he's never materialised. People used to tease me that if I opened the toys I'd probably find them stuffed with hacksaw blades. I always wondered what I'd find if I did open them, but why prisoners would try to smuggle things out I can't imagine.

There was one bloke in there who was incredibly good-looking. He couldn't have been more than twenty-five. We found out later he was a murderer. I think it was a crime of passion. We talked to him after one of the performances and remarked that he looked browner than the last time. 'It's not suntan,' he replied. 'It's all make-up. I don't think I'll be going on my holidays for a while yet.' I thought it was good he could accept the fact and joke about it.

We go to all the plays. There's one every six months. And we've been to two or three carol services. They're a very different setup. We have to get Home Office clearance to attend.

Every prisoner can go if they want, although the turnout often depends on what film is on as an alternative. The prison officers sit round the edge of the chapel with their walkie-talkies and some of them look more violent and aggressive than the prisoners. You can tell which prisoners are on remand because they wear brown prison clothing, or their own clothes. All the rest are in blue and grey. There is never a lot of room between us. Only a few feet. Some of the prisoners' friends can go up and talk to them afterwards. It's a nice atmosphere.

I found the end of the first evening difficult. All the prisoners had to go back to their cells when the play finished, but I could walk through the doors. I was free. It was hard realising that they weren't. It made me more appreciative of what I have: a nice bright room all to myself, in a pleasant, five-bedroomed house about twenty years old. The Vicarage is built in sandy-coloured brick and there's ivy growing up the front, past Dad's study and Rachel's bedroom window.

I'm glad my room's not at the front. For some reason I've never been keen on Rachel's, which is the spare room now. I don't know whether it's the trees at the side of the drive making it dark, or the fact that it looks out over the church. Prince Charles might go on about modern architecture but St Mary's is enough to turn anyone's stomach. It was Georgian originally, then it was doctored by the Victorians. It's very ugly and needs half a million to be spent on it in repairs. The trouble is that it has some kind of interest for the conservationists, though for the life of me I can't think why. Even if it was burnt down, and we have been tempted, it would have to be rebuilt, brick for brick.

It's a good job the real church is people rather than buildings. There are between three and four hundred in the congregation each week, with a core I know quite well. I have most contact with CYFA, the young people's group, who meet at the curate's house on Sunday evenings for discussions of relevant social topics.

I used to get on well with Chris, a former curate. Once I'd got over my initial shock of him working on the holiday mission in Frinton and knowing the others. Joe used to be in his group at the mission, and both my sisters attended regularly. I went once and hated it. Chris had to try really hard to persuade me to work on the mission in Wales with him. I thought it would be like Frinton. Chris listened to my views, but soon put me right. It was good being able to talk to him. He was like an older brother while he was here, but they've moved now. One of his little girls is my goddaughter. I must go and see them sometime, once the weather gets better. They're not far from the coast and I might even get to visit the sea. I love the beach and open spaces.

That's another bonus in being at the back of the house. My bedroom looks out over the garden, which is mainly lawn and silver birch trees. Beyond, there's a big stretch of allotments that must go on for nearly half a mile. I suppose we're lucky to have so much space in London, but I'm not quite so keen on all the alleyways surrounding us, or the fact that the house is set back so far from the road. The only time it's an advantage is when we have parties and there are no neighbours to complain. The rest of the time we're never sure who's around. There's a constant flow of parents to and from the school next door, people in and out of the flats opposite the end of our drive, folk taking a short cut, drunks from the pub at the end of the road. It's not at all unusual to find them relieving themselves in the churchyard. I don't think people would be quite so keen to have their wedding photos taken in certain parts if they knew what happens there when no one's around. It's quite an eye-opener living in a vicarage, especially in such a mixed area as Ealing.

Most of the kids at the school come across the footbridge from the council estate on the other side of the railway line. It's called the Trees Estate and the roads are named after trees. Almond, Sycamore, Cedar, Chestnut. I don't know whether they planted any when the estate was built and they've all been vandalised, or whether it's because there was an orchard there once. There aren't many trees around now. Not many people from that area come to church, though it's in our parish.

Our congregation comes from the more affluent sideroads off the main road. It's typical London suburbia really. There's lots of home ownership, and some fairly big houses in parts, especially in some of the roads along and behind the allotments, this side of the railway line. Neil Kinnock lives only a couple of hundred yards from the church, and the old Ealing Studios are just up the road, past the YMCA building. We have a couple of parks, Lammas and Walpole, within easy walking distance, and a very big open area, Gunnersbury Park, south of the council estate.

If I want the shops, South Ealing has lots of small ones, but Ealing Broadway has the chain stores and a big shopping precinct. The DHSS offices are there too. David was heading in that direction this morning, if I'm correct. I'm a bit more with it now, having had time to wake up gradually. Let's get this right. David and I went to Scotland on Friday, the last day of February. Saturday was 1 March. We had a marathon journey home on Sunday night. Monday, I crashed out. Tuesday, Dave went into work, but wasn't really up to it. Then he wasn't paid the amount he was promised so he walked out. Wednesday he registered as unemployed. Today must be Thursday. So . . . it must be 6 March.

That feels better. I know where I am now. If Dave has gone to sign on he could be round any time. He hates being unemployed and won't know what to do with himself. He won't want to stay stuck in his room at the hostel for long, that's for sure. I must get up and dressed.

What to wear? That's the problem. The doctor advises no trousers so that the air can circulate, because of this stupid fungal condition. That doesn't leave a lot of choice. A skimpy summer dress in March is going to look a bit ridiculous, even with a jumper. It will have to do though. So will my bikini top. I couldn't bear wearing a bra at the moment. It's a good job I'm not going anywhere. Or likely to get run over by a London bus. All I have to worry about is that Dave doesn't go getting any ideas. And if he does? Tough. He knows where I stand, or he should do by now.

CHAPTER THREE

I have made it as far as one of the settees in the lounge, opposite the wall with Grandma's military prints. Outside in the garden the birches are still bare. There is some way to go till spring is really here. The folding wooden doors between the lounge and dining room remain firmly closed. If I had the energy I could write a letter, but I haven't. That disturbed night has really knocked the stuffing out of me. It's as much as I can do to keep my eyes open to watch TV.

I hope David's feeling a bit better today. It's not like him to be under the weather. The only time I've known him to be ill was when I persuaded him to go with me to be a blood donor. I was querying a point with the doctor and the next thing I knew there were six nurses and a doctor all fussing round Dave holding his head up, giving him a bowl in case he was sick and I don't know what. And they have the cheek to call women the weaker sex. He reckoned he passed out because he'd been up all night working, but he had to have some excuse. Fainting can't be too good for the male ego.

It made me think twice, mind you. I was tempted to opt out when the doctor asked if I was still willing to give my blood. I've always hated anything to do with hospitals or blood, and it was only the crying need for blood donors that made me volunteer in the first place.

Dave's little drama wasn't the end of the story either. I didn't escape totally unscathed. I gave my blood without any problem, had the usual fifteen minutes' break and then went to see David, who was still resting. We were chatting away quite happily till one of the nurses came along and in a very loud voice asked me to move because I was making David's blood pressure rise too fast. Talk about being embarrassed. Before they let him go they told Dave to make sure he had a good night's sleep and a proper meal before he tried to give blood again. I don't think he needed telling twice.

He's quite a bloke really, with his good looks, warm brown eyes and friendly personality. He's got ambition, too. For a couple of years now he's wanted to join the police force. He respects the police and wants to do something to help people. Heaven knows where I shall end up. I've been in responsible positions as far as work is concerned and on the holiday mission, but I don't really know what I want to do with my life. My ambitions are far more frivolous. I'd like to fly in a hot-air balloon, and visit the Great Barrier Reef.

Mum probably put the idea about Australia into my head. She went there when she was three and held a koala in Sydney Zoo and other exciting things. I've seen something of the Great Barrier Reef on TV. I think it's beautiful. I'd love to see it for myself. Going up in a hot-air balloon must be thrilling. I love the sensation of wind flowing all round and at me. I like going to the top of a hill. Not the climb up so much, but standing on top, letting the air get right to me, blowing all the cobwebs away.

David and I went for a walk in Gunnersbury Park one day and asked each other about our ambitions. It was good finding out more about one another. We spend most of our time together talking, or with friends. We've found that we have quite a lot in common. He's worked on a farm, and I'm interested in farming. We both like animals. I think he likes sixties music, but I'm not sure. I definitely do. He enjoys reading, and he likes motor bikes, so he'd probably get on OK with my brother. Joe's been mad on racing cars as long as I can remember, and most of his writing is about cars.

The only thing Dave and I don't see eye to eye on is Christianity. We talk a lot about it, though, and he's even begun to read a few books on the subject. He knows how important it is to me. It's not just something I have to go along with because my father is a vicar. I've always gone to church but I date my real decision to be a follower of Christ from the age of twelve. I was away at camp and while we were there the son of my group leader fell in a river and was drowned. His body wasn't found until about a week later, but the family all stayed on at camp. Mum, dad, and his teenage sister. At the end of the holiday the camp leader asked if anyone had learned anything during the camp and the boy's sister stood up. Five days earlier her brother had died, yet she was the first to admit she had learned something. I wanted what she had got, and decided there and then to become a Christian. I trusted totally that God was in control. He loved me and was always there, more than anyone or anything else. Whatever happened.

From then on Christianity affected everything I thought or did, including sex. Dad could rest content. Sex was for marriage. Not because he said so in a book written twenty years before, but because caring, concern and commitment are values set down in the Bible. Although it was written centuries before dad's own contribution to the debate, it still has so much to say to today's society. I haven't seen anything to persuade me to question its teachings seriously. Particularly when I see the mess some people make of their lives by just doing their own thing. At college I couldn't believe how naïve the girls were about contraception, even though they were having sex.

I know a lot of people don't agree with my views, including Dave, but he respects my beliefs. I've only once found myself in a situation where a bloke could have led me astray. He said he found me incredibly attractive physically and I thought the same about him. I was very tempted to go back on everything

I believed in. It made me realise how fine the dividing line is. Since then I've been even more determined to make sure people know my decision, and the fact that I'm sticking to it. I like to have fun, but at the end of the day they know where I stand and they can like it or lump it.

Not that it has put me off men. Most of the men I count as my friends I have 'fancied' first. My name actually means flirt and I've often been called one, much to my annoyance. How are you supposed to act with the opposite sex, for heaven's sake? Nobody ever explains properly. Mum and Dad told us about the physical act, and gave us books to read on the subject. The rest I've picked up from TV, friends at school and CYFA. What puzzles me is how to work out what's going on in someone's mind, whether they're seeing me as a friend, or reading all kinds of other things into the relationship.

Take David, for instance. I hope he's not building too many castles in the air after hiring a car and taking me up to Scotland to meet his family. He's nice to be with, and I wouldn't hurt him for the world but I'm not sure marrying him would be right, even if I do indulge in the occasional fantasy of my own. I've always wanted to get married and have kids. I can't think why. I'm not all that good with small children. Babies always seem to cry when I'm around. I prefer them older – I think they ought to be born about three years old. Everyone says it's different when they're your own, so I suppose I'll have to take their word for it and trust that it's true. One day. But not yet. There's still so much David and I have to learn about one another. We may have been going out together for more than six weeks but we could so easily spoil things by getting too serious.

Scotland was great, though, and it was nice meeting his family. His mum and dad, two brothers, his sister-in-law and niece, and the black Labrador. David had told me quite a bit about them so it was good to see them, if only for a flying visit. I enjoyed our day out touring on Saturday. Everyone had told me that men in kilts or playing bagpipes were the exception rather than the norm. I saw both.

The scrape with the car that same evening wasn't quite so much fun. David had only gone into a shop for a minute when another car reversed into ours. I turned round sharply to see what happened and get the number. I knew the hire company wouldn't be too pleased if their car was damaged, and it was my money, taken out of the building society, that they had as the deposit as Dave's pay hadn't come through on time. I tried to find a pen to write down the registration number but in the end I had to rely on my memory. Unfortunately it wasn't at its best. I'd just had some cough mixture and felt a bit drowsy. Normally I revel in remembering things. It's a bit like a game. I train myself to notice details when I see shifty characters hanging around. What is he wearing? What does his jacket look like? Does he have any distinguishing marks? That kind of thing.

As soon as David got back he inspected the damage. There was a dent and a black plastic bumper had scraped along the car. We did debate going to the police but I thought they might dispute whether I could remember the number accurately enough after taking medicine, and not knowing much about cars I could only vaguely describe the shape. We found the car for ourselves later. Parked right near David's house. Dave went in to see the owner. He had a story all worked out, but his car bumper had been damaged.

That should have been enough excitement for one weekend but there was more to come. On the way home we got ourselves involved in a 'domestic'. We decided to drive back via Liverpool so I could show David where I lived for the first two and a half years of my life. We didn't leave his home till gone eleven, and managed to get ourselves lost round the back streets of Liverpool at 2 am in the morning. We were driving through Walton when we saw a man beating up a woman. David reversed back and told the man to leave her alone. The man said it was a 'matrimonial dispute' but he stopped hitting the woman and she was able to run off. David offered her a lift but she didn't want one, so we just followed her in the car till we were sure she was out of harm's way.

By this time we were totally lost, and just following diversion signs. I was beginning to get slightly bothered but amazingly we made it to Shaw Street, my old road. We had a quick look at the house but didn't hang around for long. There was a police car nearby and there was no knowing what they might make of two suspicious characters cruising round such a derelict area in the middle of the night.

David was very tired so we stopped by the docks for him to have a sleep. It wasn't any use. He couldn't relax properly so we decided it was best to go on. We made it with minutes to spare, after crawling along in the usual mayhem on the motorway in the rush hour. The car-hire man was still not very happy, but eventually he gave us our deposit back, much to our relief. If the deal had been invalid we would have had to pay by the mile and as we'd done over a thousand miles we would have been totally broke. I thought that was the end of our troubles, but as we lugged our suitcases over the racks at the tube station I dropped one of the bags. Inside it had a bottle of Irn Bru, a bright orange Scottish drink which David loves, and which went all over my clothes and mittens.

Is it any wonder I crashed out for hours, and still feel pretty rough, especially with the coughing and pain in my ribs? I haven't even had the energy to take the money back to the building society yet. I must try and make the effort tomorrow. We don't keep much cash in the house. Living in a vicarage you never know who's going to be around. Yesterday it was British Telecom, installing new phones. Now we have one in the study, one in the kitchen and one in Mum and Dad's bedroom. That will be useful when I feel in need of a bit of consolation from Jim or Chris. Jim definitely comes into the 'fancying' category. I learned early on that nothing was likely to come of it, but he still manages to make me feel good. We talk a lot and I know I can be frank with him. He has a great gift for encouraging people and often gives sound advice. Sometimes I've liked him, and sometimes I've hated him for it, but we've stayed friends.

David finds my men friends a bit hard to take at times so I'd better watch what I say when he's around. Ah, talk of the devil. There's the doorbell. I suppose I'd better answer it, even though Dad's study is next to the door. Dad has great difficulty in understanding Dave. It's not surprising, really. Dave's family live in Cumbernauld, which is near Glasgow, so everyone has a fairly broad accent, though on occasion I still tease Dave that I'm as much of a Northerner as he is. Perhaps not today. It would require too much effort.

CHAPTER FOUR

It doesn't take us long to decide what we want to do. We have a double episode of *Dallas* to watch on the video. The part where Bobby comes back in the shower. And I thought Pug had a vivid imagination! At 12.30 we switch over to *The Sullivans* on TV. The other half of *Dallas* can wait till later. David does not have much say in the matter. I like *The Sullivans*. It's a good, clean, historic soap. Quite a contrast to some of the rubbish that's put out.

We have hardly settled ourselves when there's another ring at the doorbell. A staff meeting is planned for two o'clock. Surely they're not arriving yet? It's only quarter to one. I answered the door last time; Dad can sort this one out. If I go anywhere it ought to be to the loo. I've needed to go since about eleven o'clock, but haven't got that far yet. It's nice and peaceful curled up here with David. Safe. Comfortable.

Ah well, all good things must come to an end. A workman has just walked into the room and out again. I didn't know anything else needed mending. The place seems to have been inundated with workmen for the last few months; it's about time everything was fully operational. Now a second man is coming into the room. Don't say they need to work in here. Dad never mentioned anything about it.

Something is wrong. The man is brandishing a large kitchen knife. Telling us to move. These are no workmen. I scramble to my feet and head towards the study, the direction the man is indicating. David goes to follow. Man 2 grabs him and pulls him down the corridor, hitting him about the face and head with his hands. What is happening?

In the study there are some cash boxes upturned and open on the desk and Dad is seated, with a third man holding a long knife threateningly towards him. The one I mistook for a workman is wandering around, giving instructions. He looks older than the other two but it's difficult to tell. Most of his face is concealed by a dark balaclava. Only his eyes are visible. There seems something strange about them, though I can't quite make out what it is. This is not real. *Dallas* has somehow got mixed up with the everyday. Only it's not glamorous enough for *Dallas* and far too frightening for any day I have ever known.

I sit down quickly on the nearest seat. Man 2 has bundled David into the room, and is evidently not pleased with what the others have found. He points his knife at my chin and threatens to cut my throat if Dad doesn't tell him where the money is kept. This is ridiculous. If this man wants to cut my throat he won't get very far with the knife pointing at my chin. Steady girl. Don't get carried away. Just stay calm. Dad is telling them there is no money – this is a vicarage. As if they could fail to notice. It's written in letters six inches high above the front door. Shut up Dad. Play it cool. These men are obviously hyped up, especially the two younger ones, who seem coarser, more aggressive. They're not going to listen to reason, to the voice of authority.

Man 1 diverts attention. He takes hold of my arm, saying we are going upstairs to look for jewellery. He too is armed with a kitchen knife. There is nothing for it but to lead the way. My room is opposite the top of the stairs. He looks at my few bits and pieces but throws them back on the chest of drawers, as if they're not worth his while, or he doesn't want to keep them if they're my property. He seems surprised to have found David and me at home. I have the distinct impression that he expected only to see my father.

'Remember I was kind to you,' he says. 'Don't tell the others.' The accent is London. He is stocky, potbellied, slightly shorter than me. About five foot seven, I would say. I have noticed that one of the men has lettering tattooed across the knuckles of three fingers. Something like MAR. I try to check whilst we are in Mum and Dad's room but his fingers are moving through Mum's jewellery so fast I cannot be certain. He is obviously a man who knows what he is after. A professional. Mum's gold watch, ruby cluster ring and gold chain must be worth a lot more than my jewellery, which is mainly silver. He forces open a couple of boxes and tips the drawers from the bedside cabinet onto the bed, but there is little more to interest him. He is ready to go.

Downstairs Dad and David have their trousers around their ankles and Men 2 and 3 are keeping guard. Man 2 doesn't seem to believe that Man 1 has everything. He starts to shout and swear. I hardly have time to see what is going on before I am on the move again. Being ordered upstairs at knife-point, this time by Man 2. He says he wants to check the place again, but he is pushing me towards Rachel's room. There is nothing in there, except for Scrubby and a pile of clean washing neatly folded on the bed. What can I show him? What does he want?

No. Not that. Please. He is facing me with the knife. Ordering me to undress. I pull my white V-necked jumper slowly over my head. This is the fear every woman has grown up with from the time we are old enough to be warned not to talk to strangers. With good cause. I have already experienced three unpleasant 'incidents' on the streets of London. They roll through my memory like a cartoon series, fast and fragmented. Only there is nothing to laugh about in this sequence. The first time, aged nine, I was with my brother and sister at London Zoo. I was watching the seals being fed, when a fat man came and stood behind me, pushing his hand inside my clothes and breathing heavily. It was horrible. Suffocating. I was pinned against the railings, unable to move until the crowds dispersed and I could run to find my brother.

The second time I had just left college, but I was still petrified when a man started to follow me through Walpole Park. He kept chatting, asking me to go out with him or kiss him. It was repulsive. A total stranger expecting me to share the intimacy of a kiss, not taking 'No' for an answer. When I finally made it to the gates one of them was closed. There were bushes all around. I was sure the man was going to rape me. My legs turned to jelly. How I got through the other gate I shall never know. I ran into the library next to the park and stayed there reading a book on self-defence till he was no longer anywhere to be seen.

The third incident happened on my way to work early one morning. As I began my daily walk along the alleyway two Asian lads in school uniform were coming towards me. Suddenly one ran at me and grabbed my chest as he passed. I turned around in utter amazement. He stood there, some distance away, rubbing his penis through his trousers, with a big grin on his face. He could not have been more than thirteen.

Is it any wonder women form plans in their minds about what they will do if the worst happens? I knew I would go to Jim. He would help me. Now the worst is happening but it is not in the dark alleyway I have always imagined. It is here in my own home. I have taken as long as I dare undressing. The man is pulling down his trousers, pushing me to my knees in front of him. I once saw some Swedish playing cards that a resident at the YMCA had. I found them totally disgusting, but quite educational. What this man is telling me to do is even more disgusting. This would not happen in a dark alleyway even in the most distressing nightmare. I can feel tears welling in my eyes. 'Don't you dare cry,' the man threatens.

I blink back the tears and do as he demands. I am coughing

and retching but how can you argue with a man who has erratic behaviour and a large knife?

He orders me on to the bed, knocking Mum's neatly ironed washing to the floor. There are more instructions. Things I have never read about in textbooks. Or heard discussed at youth groups. This has nothing to do with the fulfilment of a committed relationship, special and complete. It is sordid, dirty, violent, with a total stranger who reeks of stale tobacco and beer like an old pub. I feel sick. Physically and emotionally. All I can do is pray, 'God let me come out of this alive.'

I am conscious of movement on the landing. The other men are outside with Dad and Dave.

'We didn't come here for this,' one of them protests.

Man 2 ignores them. He pushes me out of the spare room, along the corridor, and into my bedroom. A woman in the alleyway outside looks up at the window. I will her to phone the police, fire brigade, anyone. Please. Help. Can't she see the fear written all over my face? Doesn't she wonder why I am standing starkers in the middle of the day, in full view?

Man 2 launches into a fresh onslaught, this time on my own bed. The thought that Dad and Dave are upstairs in the spare room is making me even more tense. I am being attacked from all angles, though Man 2 has an extremely limited vocabulary of four-letter words to express his demands. I switch off emotionally. This must be the kind of thing they put in pornographic movies, activities that take place in seamy studios behind darkened windows. Not in full daylight in my own room with the man's two accomplices wandering in and out at will.

A phone rings but remains unanswered. The emergency services are not rushing to my aid. I must help myself. The knife is on the edge of the bed. Man 2 is fully occupied. If I can edge the knife with my knee. Push it onto the floor, like so. Now, Man 1, show what you are made of. You were kind to me once. Come and get the knife. Quickly, before he sees that it has fallen.

Now I need them, they are not there. Man 2 notices the knife. He grabs it and orders me into a different position. There is blood on the sheet. In my mouth. My blood. So much for trying to remain a virgin, saving myself for my wedding night. Who will want me now? Will I ever be able to live with myself after these depravities? I am retching again. I can't stand the sight of blood, let alone the taste, and am sickened by the acts this man seems to want me to enjoy. My body has become an object. A machine. It must stay like that if I am to survive.

I concentrate on details about the men. This one must be six foot. Sturdy. He has dark, greasy hair with dandruff. A steel-blue padded jacket with patches on the shoulders, probably suede. Flaky, scabbed skin on his thigh. A pink rubber washing-up glove on one of his hands, turned down about the wrist. A tattoo like some kind of spider's web on the part of his arm that shows.

The other men are back now that it is too late. One uses a name. Gary . . . Wayne . . . Jason. Something modern. I am not sure. Man 1 is getting edgy. He turns on Man 3 for leaving Dad and Dave unattended in the spare room. Man 2 is not happy either. Evidently I am not giving him enough satisfaction. He tells me to turn on to my stomach. Apologising for what he is about to do. This is worse. Far worse. I did not think such things were possible. Words won't ever explain how I feel.

Man 3 rifles through my jewellery, unperturbed by my anguish or the threats. He has put on my mittens to avoid leaving fingerprints. Concentrate on him, girl. Don't think what the other one is doing. Man 3 must have small hands. The mittens hardly fit me, especially since the Irn Bru spilt over them. Small hands. Slim build. Hair straggly at the back, short on top. Most likely the remains of a crew cut. Unnatural colour, possibly highlighted. A stubbly chin, as though he hasn't shaved. Two knives hang from his belt, one a big-bladed butcher's knife, the other more like a black-handled kitchen knife.

Man 2 is changing techniques again. He has not let go of his knife. Far from it. He is pointing it towards me. But not at my chin this time. Earlier I prayed 'Lord, let me live.' Now my cry is 'Let me have children.' If this man slashes my inside, that will be the end of all my dreams. Thankfully my prayer is answered. He turns the knife, and uses the handle instead. It doesn't work. Nothing can break through the mechanical barrier I have built around myself. He has taken my body against my will, against my principles. No way is he going to have my co-operation.

Man 1 is still restless. He knows that people are coming and wants to go. I have the distinct impression he is beginning to panic, but why has he fetched Dad's cricket bat from the garage? I have heard moans coming from the spare room. Now there is a new sound. Like a ball hitting the bat. Someone is telling David to shut up. It doesn't seem to register. The more he groans the more he gets hit. 'Leave him alone,' I beg. What has he done? We were only watching TV.

There are no more sounds. I don't know which is worse, the shouts, or this terrible silence. Man 2 seems not to care. His mind is still turned in one direction. He says Man 3 looks hungry, hungry for sex. Man 3 agrees with him. He draws the curtains and joins in the assault.

Oh Mum. All those hours you spent watching, waiting. Trying to protect us. Hanging over the gate if we were more than a few minutes late. Letting Pug and me go down to the shops only if we were together until we were eleven or twelve. Who could have foreseen this happening? With Dad and Dave only yards away. Powerless to do anything.

I am still retching. The men's demands are impossible. Even they seem to be getting the message at last. Man 3 produces a bottle of vodka. The one Pug bought herself, if I am not mistaken. They offer me some. Several times. They have just got to be joking.

Man 3 asks if it is my 'first time' and seems to take great

delight when he finds it is. They want to know whether it's my name on the wall. Do I have to answer? Now they know another intimate detail about me. The essence of my identity. I haven't a clue to theirs apart from that modern-sounding name, which for the life of me I can't remember.

Man 2 throws the duvet on top of me, and tells me to cover myself up. I do not need telling again. Man 3 is trying to tie me up with a towel but is having great problems. He is still wearing my mittens, and towels are not the easiest of things to knot. He looks round for something else. There is a length of washing line for skipping, on my washing basket. I hurriedly suggest that. I might stand a chance of escaping then. If he uses nylon wool I shall never get out of it. I remember the problems we had when we used to play cowboys and Indians. Man 3 does as I suggest and between them, he and Man 2 somehow manage to tie my wrists and ankles together.

At last I am alone. I know I can get one of my feet free but I can still hear the men walking around. In and out of the spare room, down the stairs, into the hall. One of them is saying, 'No. We can't take that. It's too big.' The front door slams. My feet are already free, and one of my hands. I pick up the towel from the floor and wrap it round me. Someone has gone. Have all three? I will take the risk. I must find out what they have done to Dad and Dave. I can't hear any sounds. I walk slowly along the corridor. I hate pain and the thought of finding a dead body petrifies me. The door to the spare room is shut. What will I find when I manage to open it?

CHAPTER FIVE

Dad and Dave are obviously badly hurt but still alive. The relief is enormous. The decision who to help first is more tricky. Dad is lying face down on the floor, his head almost hidden beside a chair, and his wrists tied behind him with a belt. David has blood pouring down the whole of one side of his face. The men have tipped green Radox crystals on to the wounds. The empty box is lying on the floor. The pain he must be suffering does not bear thinking about. He is tied by the lead of my cassette recorder, wrists to ankles from behind, and is hurling himself round the room. He'll do himself further injury if he doesn't calm down. I still have the rope around my arms but leave that to try to help him. Once the first couple of knots are undone he jumps his feet through the lead, rips the end of the flex off and throws himself onto the bed, sobbing. I turn my attention to Dad. He seems to be breathing. Just. I untie his hands and turn him over. The back of his head is hurting. He thinks he has been shot but there is no sign of blood.

I have done all I can for them. Now I must get medical help. The phone in Mum and Dad's bedroom is nearest, but the flex has been cut. British Telecom are not going to be pleased after putting it in only yesterday. I run downstairs. The study phone is also out of action. Don't let them have done anything to the one in the kitchen. Please.

Thankfully it is untouched. I dial 999. I have always wondered how the operator responds. Now I have my answer.

'Which service do you require?'

'Police and ambulance.' Fast.

Name? Address? Reason for the call?

Rape is mentioned from the word go. I am only giving the briefest details but it seems to be taking an eternity. At last the girl on the switchboard knows all she needs. I can go back upstairs to Dad and David. Dad wants to know if I am all right, then asks, 'Did they?' There is no avoiding an answer. It must be obvious from the state I am in. He says he is sorry. I have no feelings. Only a numbness where I think they should be.

I hear sirens coming in our direction, then going away again. Come on, come on. Why is it taking so long? I thought it was supposed to be an emergency service. Does one of us have to die before we get any action? The staff will be coming for that meeting at two o'clock. It is now one forty-five. I must phone and warn them it will have to be cancelled. I dial the numbers mechanically, still functioning on auto pilot. It is no use. Nobody is home.

Sirens again. Coming nearer. I mustn't bank on it, not yet. Now. It's OK. They are coming into our turning, ringing the doorbell. A big policeman stands on the doorstep. Several others are following him up the path and the ambulance is not far behind. They apologise for the delay; they had taken a wrong turning. Can I tell them where the others are? What happened? Shall we go into the lounge?

I still have only a towel wrapped round me, and must look a total mess. I can feel the blood drying round my mouth, pulling the skin taut. I must not wash it off, or go to the loo, although I've been dying to go for hours. All those police programmes on TV have served their purpose; I have picked up a bit of useful information along the way. I know that the police will want as much evidence as possible.

A couple of the younger officers seemed a bit taken aback

when they first arrived, but the presence of the police is calming, reassuring. They know what to do. The right things to ask. Someone interrupts the questioning. David is on his way to hospital. I didn't even know they had taken him out. A second ambulance has been called. Have we got a bowl somewhere? Dad is being sick. The ambulance men won't appreciate a mess all over the ambulance floor. The kitchen is Mum's domain. We hardly ever do anything in there, except make coffee for friends and wash up at Christmas, but I manage to find a bowl from somewhere. Dad is taken out strapped in a chair. The police ask if I would like to find something warm to put around me, and would I prefer to go to the hospital or the police station for the examination? That's a surprise. I didn't know I could have a choice. I hadn't expected to go to hospital but it seems the best option.

David's sheepskin coat is lying on the settee. I pick it up and wrap it around me. It is warm and big and some form of security as I prepare to face the outside world. The curates, Eric and Ian, turn up just as we are about to leave, and a few neighbours and passers-by have appeared to see what is going on. Do they have to see me in this state? Why are they stopping now? Where were they when I needed them?

My legs are like jelly as we walk down the drive. If the police weren't holding on to me I am sure I would collapse. Somehow we make it to the ambulance. The door slams shut. We are on our way. A policeman blocks my view of Dad, much to my relief. I do not relish the thought of watching him being sick. The police are not wasting any time. They need answers to another set of questions. Who else lives in the house? Where are they?

I know I must answer their questions coherently, but that one nearly throws me. Mum. Pug. Someone has to break the news to them. They are both still at work. Don't tell Pug too much. She's my twin. It might be best if you let Mum explain what has happened when she gets to the hospital. A police car rushes past us. Sirens blaring. They are in a hurry to get somewhere. Let's hope they don't get lost again. We turn off the main road and up a ramp to Ealing Hospital. The main entrance is not on the ground floor. It's a very confusing building. On at least two occasions I've ended up on the wrong floor. I nearly went into the mortuary one day by mistake. I refused to go near the place for ages afterwards. It's not much to look at either, just a vast expanse of grey concrete. Not exactly conducive to making people feel better.

A wheelchair is waiting for me when the ambulance pulls to a halt. I am rushed along blue-walled corridors into a cubicle. The police protest. I need to be in a room. Eventually someone manages to find an empty examination room. Nurses take my temperature, pulse and blood pressure. My towel and David's coat are whisked away for forensic tests. I am given a hospital gown and a blanket to lie under, and then introduced to two policewomen. They must have been in the car that overtook us. One of them asks if I can give a brief description of the men and the incident while they are waiting for the police doctor. First I must know about Dad and David. How are they? Someone tells me David has been transferred to Charing Cross Hospital. They are very worried about him, and Charing Cross has a more specialised unit. I don't know if it is good news or bad.

It takes me far less time to make up my mind about the doctor when he starts to examine me. I have swabs taken from my throat, skin, anus and vagina. My throat is already sore. Having someone poking around is agony and the doctor is not exactly gentle. He needs hair from my head and pubic area. One that has come out naturally and one that he has to pull. To him it is just a routine examination. He seems entirely unaware that any remaining shreds of self-confidence are being chopped away as remorselessly as the samples he is now taking from my fingernails. Chop. Chop. Hack away. Don't worry about trying to keep a normal shape. One more little indignity won't make any difference.

To make matters worse his knowledge of English is very limited. He doesn't seem to understand what I am saying, and it feels as though he is twisting my words. It's as if he's implying it was my fault. 'Come on. You asked for it.' That kind of thing. I don't mind the police questioning if it helps to get the men caught, but this is a different proposition. He is asking intimate questions with a smile on his face. I would like to transfer it to the back of his head.

A policewoman intervenes. She tries to explain what has happened. He still doesn't seem able to understand. Or believe the evidence of his own eyes. The bruises. The bleeding. I am furious. The police had offered me a woman doctor, but I was prepared to go along with whatever would make it easier for them. This is not helping me much, however. They should try taking my blood pressure now.

I've given the policewomen details of David's family and a description of the men, though I don't know how, with all that's been going on. Now one of them is radioing it in. If they've finished, please can I go to the loo. I am getting desperate. A nurse brings a disposable bowl. She suggests turning on a tap to encourage me. I don't think I need any encouragement. I am wrong. My body is too tense. First the rape. Then finding Dad and David. The examination is the final straw. I know it has to be done, that it is part and parcel of reporting rape. Could it not be done with a little more compassion? More appreciation of what a woman has already undergone? I have had enough. All I want are my own clothes and to be left alone. It is not to be. The policewoman returns and tells me that Mum is outside. Before I see anyone I must tidy myself up. The policewoman agrees. I am allowed to wash my hands and face and swill my mouth out. At last.

Mum has been collected from work by Ian and has more up-to-date news of Dad. It is good to see her and get a reassuring hug. Pug comes next. The police have done as I asked and let Mum break the news to her. She seems to be taking it all right. No one howls or throws a wobbly. We're a restrained family. Stiff upper lip and all that. The conversation is mainly about Dad and David, and what has been stolen. There isn't much to say about the actual attack. They know vaguely what has happened but I have no intention of going into details. That is more than anyone could handle.

Joe is next on the scene. It's great to see him after being so conscious of missing him earlier in the day. It means I get another hug, too. I said it was good having a big brother. Being part of the church family isn't bad either. Already messages of love and concern are beginning to creep in via different sources. News certainly spreads fast. I am quite impressed when we get a visit from the local bishop, complete in priestly purple.

I still haven't got my clothes. Pug can collect them. She will know what I need. A couple of police officers drive her to the Vicarage. It is not a good move. They hit the rush hour and take hours going the couple of miles up the road and back. The police are waiting to take me to the new rape suite at Brentford Police Station. I am just as anxious to be going. When Pug gets back I bundle into my clothes, unaware of what she might be feeling. When we are out of earshot a police officer has to warn me that Pug saw the blood on the sheet in my room and was pretty distressed. That is just the kind of thing I was dreading might happen. I want to spare her as many of the gory details as I possibly can.

There is no chance to correct it now. The police are on the move. It's time to go. As we walk out into the cold night air I forget everything else as I am once more overtaken by a strong desire to go to the loo. Brentford is more than a mile down the road. Will we make it in time?

The WDI asks what we want to eat. Ever since I watched the film *Kramer vs Kramer* and saw the little boy Billy turned off the food he was eating when his mum and dad told him they were getting divorced I have been wary about what I eat in times of stress. McDonald's is already taboo. I don't want other favourites to follow a similar fate. In the end I opt for fish and chips. I don't think anything will ever turn me off them.

Drink is more of a problem. I'm not a tea or coffee drinker and I certainly don't want alcohol. The first time I ever had brandy I was in a pub in North Wales, and all my friends were laughing at me. Earlier that week I had walked home holding hands with one of the Welsh lads and he told his mates we were going out together. I said most emphatically that we were not. I didn't realise if you held hands with a bloke it meant you were going out with him. The lads thought it was very funny but I found it difficult to handle. After that I decided if ever I was going to drink I was going to make sure it was when I was happy. I wasn't ever going to resort to it as a means of picking myself up. It's far too easy to become addicted to it. Besides, the men had offered me alcohol. I settle for a Coke.

The rape suite at Brentford is a small unit away from the main building. I have some idea what to expect because it was shown on television about a month ago when it was opened. Even so, I am impressed by the relaxed atmosphere, which is totally unlike a normal police station. The interview room is very peaceful, tastefully decorated in subtle browns and creams. It is 'user-friendly', carpeted, with soft, comfortable seats, and pictures on the walls. There is even a coffee machine and kettle for making tea for those who actually like the stuff. I'm more interested in the bath/shower room which I am promised I can use later. The loo I make use of straightaway. At long last my body is able to relax sufficiently, although blood is still coming from my hymen.

Back in the interview room, I am introduced to the man who is to be in charge of the case. He is able to give me updates on the others. Dad has a fractured skull and a black eye. David has a fractured skull, a small blood clot on the brain, a perforated eardrum and a lot of bruising.

The fish and chips arrive and before I have finished my meal we begin the statement. I don't object. I will do anything I can to get these men caught. I feel a bit sick reliving the actual rape, especially having to talk slowly so that it can all be written down, but other than that it's OK. It's as though it isn't me speaking. I'm still on remote control.

The police help enormously. They take time to be accurate and know exactly what they are talking about, even if I don't. Words like erection, ejaculation, buggery and oral sex are not ones I have used before. Until a few hours ago I knew very little about how the male reproductive organs work when excited so I have a quick sex-education lesson, much to my embarrassment. I feel so naïve not knowing much about the mechanics or the right words to use. The police, male and female, take it all in their stride. I can laugh with them. They are sympathetic, caring, professional. A bit like concerned friends, but without the emotional involvement.

The statement is obviously going to take a long time but it is not upsetting me to talk. On the contrary. I know that it has to be done and that whatever I can remember may help, so I am concentrating as hard as I can. Every so often the man in charge of the case pops in, although there is no real contact with the main police station apart from a telephone. The police are amazed by my attention to detail. One of them tells me I have a photographic memory, which is good for them but may not be so good for me. It means I might remember the details much longer. They seem to think the whole thing horrific, and want to nail the men as soon as possible.

Mum phones to see how we are getting on. We are not allowed into the house yet so arrangements have been made for us to stay at Eric's house for the night. By ten thirty we have all had enough. The idea of a shower is abandoned. I can have a bath at Eric's house. Please God.

In the car I am offered tablets to help me sleep. I refuse. The only time I took a sleeping tablet I was awake far longer than I would have been without it. Besides, I have no more intention of becoming dependent on drugs than I have on alcohol. I have heard that one in six women take tranquillisers at some stage in their lives and I don't intend adding to the numbers. All I want is a bath to get rid of the smell of stale smoke from the men. It feels as though it is embedded in my hair , and nostrils. I want to get the smell out of my head, be clean again.

I ask Mum if she could get some TCP and Vicks vapour rub as my throat and chest are very sore. Thankfully there is a 7 – 11 shop nearby and Eric drives her up to it. When she returns I wash my mouth with the TCP, then pour the rest in the bath and over my hair, trying to disinfect myself. After I have finished, Mum washes my hair properly, and someone manages to find a hairdryer and a plug so that it can be dried thoroughly, before I catch my death of cold. I feel almost human again. Better. Cleaner.

Apparently the phone has been ringing all evening and the attack has made it to the late news headlines on BBC and ITN. The police have already advised us to say nothing to reporters so we are on our guard. Just before midnight the phone rings again. Someone from the deanery is asking about us. Mum does not recognise the name and is very wary. The caller receives a curt reply. It serves him right, whoever he is. If he had any sense he would wait until morning. It's been a long day, and we all need rest.

It is a long time coming. My ribs are incredibly sore and I miss my beanbag to relieve the pressure. However hard I try, I cannot stop my mind going back to that terrible hour. The violence of the attack. The extent. All the sordid details. This is no use. I must think of something more positive. The chorus of a song I heard at Greenbelt, a big Christian festival of the arts, creeps into my mind:

Bread of life, bread of life,
All things made new,
Bread and wine, bread and wine
We feed on you.

I sing the words quietly to myself every time I wake up and am so grateful for their reassurance. I will be made new. It says all things. Not all things excluding rape victims. Which is rather how I feel.

CHAPTER SIX

We are woken at seven thirty by the first phone call of the day. None of us have had a brilliant night's sleep and the journalist at the end of the line does not stay there long. I grab the phone before anybody else can call in. There are two people I particularly want to tell before they hear it from any other source.

In my hurry I forget that it is Jim's day off and get him out of bed to answer the phone. Hardly a good beginning. When I ask if he has heard the news he goes into a long explanation about missing it last night and not being sufficiently awake this morning to have switched it on. Why can't he just say 'No'? It would make life a lot easier. Eventually he realises that there must be a reason for me to ring so early in the morning to enquire about his viewing habits, and asks 'Why?'

While I am explaining the paperboy delivers *The Times*. There is a small paragraph on page two. Jim is stunned but he sounds basically all right. That's one less to be concerned about. The other friend is a different proposition. Unfortunately he has already been told and has had the whole night to worry. The very thing I was trying to avoid. He sounds dreadful. I try to reassure him that I am all right but he is near to tears and hardly able to talk.

Mum is next to the phone. She wants to ring the hospitals. Dad's condition is about the same. David is still 'critical'. He keeps slipping in and out of a coma. I want to see him but I'm afraid of how he might react. What if the thought of me makes him physically sick? Or he doesn't want to see me? Breakfast interrupts that line of thought, and after breakfast Pug arrives with her fiancé. She has been staying with some friends about a mile away but has had a very rough night. She seems in a worse state than me. Seeing the headlines splashed all over the tabloid newspapers hasn't helped. Maybe a brisk walk back home will ease the tension?

The Vicarage is already buzzing with police. They have taken the fingerprints from downstairs so we are allowed in as long as we don't touch anything. The WDI takes me upstairs to clarify the rooms I mention in my statement. When that is done, Mum, Pug and I are glad to get away. I want to go up to the YMCA to collect some bits for David, then I am going back to Brentford to finish the statement. It is not a pleasant thought. There are so many things I must force myself to remember, details I would rather forget. A woman is coming towards us. She used to cut our hair and has been looking for us. She says how sorry she is, then bursts into tears on Mum's shoulder. It's a strange sensation to have someone crying for me when I am completely dry-eyed. I daren't cry. I don't know who is more shocked. She because I am not in tears, or me because she is. I am touched by her concern but worried about how the other two are taking it.

Eventually we make our excuses and head for the YMCA. They are not expecting us. Nobody seems to know what to say. I know the feeling. My friend Shirley tells us they have already taken some of David's clothes up to the hospital, so I just collect some deodorant, his teddy bear and Filofax. A freelance photographer has been hanging around but he has no idea of our identity and we manage to avoid him.

We are not so lucky when we get back home. The press photographers have begun to arrive and they are taking photos of everything that moves. The police are guarding the gate so that they aren't actually allowed on the premises, but they are making their presence very obvious. When we are ready to leave for Brentford I am told to hide under a blanket. I do not appreciate the suggestion. I have seen it happening to accused people in the past, but rarely to the victims. Why should I be ashamed to show my face? I've done nothing to feel guilty about. The police explain that it's for my own protection. Everyone will be screaming for a story. It makes sense. Already the headlines include such gems as 'FIEND RAPES VICAR'S DAUGHTER'. 'VICAR SEES DAUGHTER RAPED'. Reluctantly I agree to go under the blanket.

We go into Brentford the back way, just in case. The WDI reads through the statement I made last night to refresh my memory. Several hours and fifteen sides further on it is finished. There are twenty-three pages of descriptions of people, events and missing property. The lost belongings are a minor irritant. The only things I know for sure that have been taken are the rented video, including the episode of *Dallas*, and my purse with the money I was supposed to be taking back to the building society. Mum is giving the police details of her jewellery. Besides her watch and ring, her pendant with a hologram of a green spider and a real seahorse set in gold which she bought in the States have disappeared. Grandma's MBE and a locket with a picture of Mum's dad and grandfather are also missing. They all have sentimental value, but that is nothing compared to the emotional upheaval. I have no hesitation signing that I want these men prosecuted and that I am willing to give evidence in court. It is only right. They have done wrong; they must be punished. Otherwise, what is to stop them repeating their crimes?

Rachel has arrived by the time we get back to the Vicarage. She helps us all relax by recounting a 'foot in mouth' comment she made the previous evening. She had been at a conference when she was told the news and couldn't get away. We were obviously foremost in her mind, however, and she knew she would probably have a disturbed night. Before going to bed she warned her roommate: 'If I can't get to sleep, hit me over the head with something hard.' For a moment neither of them realised what she had said, but when they did they both creased up laughing. We follow suit. It's the only way to react to things like that. It does us all a power of good.

Rachel's husband, Chris, is coming down tonight. So is Jim. Meanwhile Rachel is ready to act as chauffeur. I am not allowed to go out on my own, but she is willing to put herself at my disposal. Where would madam like to go first?

I opt to visit David. We have been warned that the hospital has been swarming with pressmen but thankfully there are none in sight when I arrive. Maybe the policeman on duty outside the door has frightened them all off. One of them has to stay there until David is able to give his statement. Inside I feel more knotted than the ropes the men used to tie my wrists. The girl that David knew has been defiled, changed, and there was nothing he could do to prevent it. Will he reject me? What will he look like? If he's surrounded by drips and all kinds of medical equipment I might follow in his footsteps and end up in a heap on the floor.

The sister helps us to feel at ease. She is very friendly and says I can come in any time of the day or night. If I want someone to talk to, they are there. It is comforting but I still clutch David's teddy bear tightly as slowly I follow her into the ward. Everyone seems to be in a coma or seriously ill and there are tubes and pipes all over the place. David is no exception. He is lying flat out in bed with the sides up to stop him falling out. There is still dried blood on his face, and a drip is attached to his arm. Not a pretty sight. The nurses have cleaned off the Radox, but I doubt if I will ever again be able to associate it with relaxation. The bruises from the cricket bat are beginning to fade but I can still see the shape of the cricket bat where he was hit. A bit like burn marks. I want to cry but my eyes stay glassy.

David drifts in and out of consciousness. He is not able to say much but he manages to take hold of my hand. He wants to know how long he has been in hospital. He thinks he's been there two weeks and wants to discharge himself. At one stage he manages to lift up the sheet and reveal to the world what he is not wearing. He hasn't rejected me. I could pick him up and hug him and never put him down.

Dad is in a room of his own at Ealing Hospital. He too has a drip. One eye is black, the other is affected by oedema caused by trauma. It looks revolting. His head is still sore and his speech slightly slurred. My sister does most of the talking. Thankfully. I haven't a clue what to say. I am angry that he has not been able to protect me. All that hype about men being the protectors seems to have flown out of the window overnight. I am grateful that he appears to tire quickly and we do not have to stay long. I am in no hurry to come again.

The sight of the dining-room table at the Vicarage revives me. It is covered in flowers. There are five bunches from the church in Fulham, one from my old school, and one from Russell and Bromley, where I worked for a time. The messages on the cards are full of hope. I am very moved by the thoughts and prayers, and by the beauty of the flowers.

People just seem to be doing all they can to ease the pressures. Someone from church is taking the washing. Others are making food and bringing it round. Or so the rest of the family tell me. I hardly have time to think, let alone eat. Mum appreciates it, though. There are a lot of people at home suddenly. Me. Rachel. Joe. Pug. Dave. Chris and Jim are due to arrive any time. Various people are flitting in and out. The police are on duty at the gate. The light at the end of the alleyway is broken so for a while they are going to stay on duty at night as well.

It has been another long day but I cannot unwind yet. Everyone else has had their fingerprints taken. Now it is my turn. There is one very large print on the wall and they want to find out who made it. Not an easy task in a vicarage; so many people have visited over the last few months. Next comes the photofit man. I have always wanted to do a photofit, it looks so easy. I soon discover how wrong I am. It's one of the hardest things I have ever had to do. I sit there, trying to eat my dinner and choose between fifty different pairs of eyes, with doorbells going, flowers arriving and the phone ringing. Constant interruptions.

I have to pick whichever features seem closest, then the man lays them on to the shape of a face. It's all in black and white but I have to tell him the colour of eyes and hair. One of the most difficult parts is the hair. Man 3 had tinted hair, but they didn't seem to have tinted hairstyles when this kit was made up so we have to draw in the light bits. We spend hours on one, then I have to say what percentage of accuracy the pictures have. I expect to have a mental block on the rapist, but that one ends up being the best. The final result looks a bit like the boy who gave me my first kiss, but I don't think he would be flattered.

I am itching for it all to be finished. Jim has arrived and I am longing to see him. The police have other ideas. They want to know if I would be willing to try hypnotherapy to help me remember the name that was used during the attack. It's bugging me too, and I want to help them all I can, but there is no way they are going to use hypnosis. I don't want someone delving into my mind when I'm not in a state of consciousness. I've given them twenty-three pages of information. That will have to be sufficient.

After more than two hours the photofits are finished. I have a long hug with Jim, but we cannot talk yet. Pug has been to a special prayer meeting they have been holding in church. She tells me one of the ladies was particularly distressed all through the meeting. I phone to tell her I am all right. She sheds a few more tears to think I am concerned about her. I wish I could ring up everyone. The press reports are alarming people. The media certainly make a meal out of things like this.

Every news station seems to be reporting it. We have even made the World Service. Jim says that as soon as he put the phone down this morning he had five calls in succession from people who were worried because they had heard what had happened. Certain friends seem to have become focal points for passing on news and reassurance. It's not much use people trying to phone here. The lines are almost constantly engaged.

Jim reckons he coped with the calls on auto pilot, and then cried when he came off the phone. It's good to be able to talk at last. I need have no inhibitions with him. We go up to my room and I tell him everything that happened. He helps me to face up to all that has been used and abused by the men. I am determined not to let them win and the session of 'ghost busting' manages to dispel any feelings of resentment or hatred that I could have towards my room. Jim came from Southport in Lancashire originally, and the first dialect I ever learned to speak was Scouse so we spend about two hours letting it rip. I wouldn't say it's the politest of conversations, but it's a relief to get things out of my system, however crude it might sound. It's a case of 'you either laugh or cry' and laughing is by far the most enjoyable. Even if I do have to hold my ribcage to stop it from hurting.

Time has had little real meaning, but I have lived over twenty-four hours since the event. I have been home one minute, in the police station or hospital the next. I have seen snippets of the news on TV, heard other bits on radio, read many interesting but not always accurate accounts of events, and watched flowers come flooding through the door in the arms of policemen. Now it is one o'clock. The day is coming to an end and I am exhausted. Thanks to Jim the fear of my room has gone. The policeman stands firm at the end of the drive, and the words of the song are still close to the surface of my mind. I can sleep in peace.

CHAPTER SEVEN

Saturday passes in a blur. There is so much to think about, so many things to do. The attack is still making front-page news, although this time the papers are concentrating more on the descriptions and photofits of the men. Everyone seems amazed at the amount of detail I have remembered. Let's just hope it helps to catch the people involved. Fast. The police certainly sound confident enough. If they get as big a response as we are receiving through the post, they should be OK. The postman arrived with the good wishes of the post office and about eight inches of post this morning. It took four people forty-five minutes just to open it and take the stamps off to send to charity. The post office must have been working overtime to interpret some of the addresses. Lots just had 'The Vicarage, Ealing', but they still managed to arrive.

People's generosity is overwhelming. We haven't done anything particularly impressive yet all these things keep rolling in. There are cards, letters, presents, money, chocolates, plants, offers of people's homes for a holiday, House of Commons wine, fluffy toys. Poor Scrubby has taken a battering. David bled over his ear. He looks very sorry for himself in comparison with the new animals, but I have no intention of parting with him. Or the chocolates. Pug and I will soon make those disappear. Dad will appreciate the wine with a good meal once he's fitter. He'd just received two bottles of champagne for encouraging Joe to join Diner's Club when the men interrupted everything on Thursday morning. While they were demanding money, Dad was willing them not to notice his champagne.

At the moment the letters should be enough to keep him occupied. He's had correspondence from Mrs Thatcher, Neil Kinnock, archbishops and all kinds of VIPs. It's not every day a clergyman gets a letter from the Prime Minister. Or from the leader of the Opposition, even if he does live just around the corner. Most of the letters are encouraging. Some offer help, others say they are praying for us. Often they are from people who have themselves been raped or attacked. One elderly lady said she was attacked in her twenties and still hasn't got over it. It is not a comforting thought. I do not want to know that it could take more than sixty years to recover. The correspondence from the prison fraternity is more comforting. Many are genuinely appalled at what has happened and express horror and sadness. A few sent us pictures or photos that are special to them. I find it very touching to receive gifts from these men who have very little they can give.

A phrase that appears quite regularly in the letters is 'I don't know what to say'. If it's any comfort to anyone, neither do I. A friend told me years ago how inadequate he had felt when his girlfriend was raped. He's obviously remembered that conversation because he's sent some flowers, and a card with the message, 'I don't know what to say.' He didn't come in. He just left it with the policeman at the gate. That's OK. I know he cares but doesn't want to impose. As long as he's not letting his imagination run away with him, and thinking things are worse than they are.

I want everyone to know that they don't need to worry about me. I'm not falling to pieces. On the contrary. I think some people are a bit shocked by my reactions. They don't expect to find me laughing and joking. They seem to think I should be sitting in a permanent puddle or something.

Pug has taken some photographs to prove I am still very

much alive and kicking. The flowers form the background. They are so spectacular we must have some kind of record. All our buckets and vases are in use and we've started on the church's now. It's almost got to the stage of putting bunches in the bath. Before long they will have taken over the whole house. I make one stipulation about the photos. They must not be too sombre. The only time I have seen a picture of someone surrounded by flowers was one taken of Pete only days before he died. I hated it. I wanted to remember him how he was. If anyone is going to take a photo of me in a similar setting it has to be full of life. Enough people are panicking about me already.

I'm amazed how many people have guessed that it's me. Though I suppose it's hardly surprising. The papers haven't actually published my name but there's enough information floating around to leave people in little doubt that the person who was raped is me. Michael Saward only has three daughters, so that limits the possibilities. The papers have also printed various other details, like my boyfriend's job and the name of my twin sister. Half a dozen people thought it might be Pug. Everyone else seems to have worked it out to be me.

I keep trying to carry on as normal in spite of all the attention, but nothing is normal. Chris is arranging flowers and doing the housework, Pug's David is cooking the meals, and Joe is dealing with the press; Jim is the shoulder to lean on. He is helping us all on a pastoral level. It's easier to talk to him. He's neutral, acceptable. He doesn't have the emotional ties.

In the afternoon Pug and I go to see my David. His condition has improved a little and we are able to spend longer with him. Pug has bought some chocolates for him to give to his mum. Tomorrow is Mothering Sunday and his mum and dad are coming down to see him. I don't know that it has sunk in, but we leave the chocolates by his bed. Every half-hour or so the nurses come round to ask him who he is, where he is, where he lives and so on. Not being a Londoner and unfamiliar with the area round the hospital he's not really sure, though he remembers my phone number easily enough. He hates the constant questioning and is getting very bored. He has been moved to the end of the ward, but is not allowed to read the newspapers or watch TV until he has made his statement. Time must seem endless. There's very little else he can do in his present condition.

His parents are driven down from Scotland overnight by a friend. They arrive on Sunday morning and are very concerned about David. The news was broken to them badly so they are not going to rest until they have seen him for themselves. They are going to join us for morning worship first, though. Today being Mothering Sunday, the church will be packed, but nothing is going to stop me from worshipping my God. Mum has asked the press to leave us alone. Pug and I have rung various clerical friends asking for their support in prayer. Someone has arranged that a statement from the Bishop of Willesden will be read during the service, followed by one from the family. Then we will enter through the side door during the first hymn.

With both families and friends from church, there are about fourteen in our group. People talk about safety in numbers but I still feel very vulnerable and exposed as we walk out of the front door and the cameras start clicking. The press have totally disregarded Mum's request. I don't think I've ever been photographed so much in my life. They've even got a long-distance camera in a room of the pub overlooking our drive. It's more like a press conference than two families going to church on Sunday morning.

As we expected, the church is full. There's the usual crowd for Mothering Sunday, plus some extras who have come to support us. Or get filmed for the news. The cameras stay outside. Inside it's the turn of the reporters, who are noting everything. Much of the service flows over me but the love that is shown is remarkable. I know that all over the world Christians are praying for me. In amongst the confusion, the pain, the feeling of being constantly busy, I am experiencing the greatest sense of peace and joy I have ever known. The prayers are working and I am being filled with the strength to carry on.

I am not in turmoil. I am not shrieking 'God, why?' My constant prayer is simply 'Get me through'. I know that God will not push me further than I can take, although we may have a few disputes on the limits He sets at times. At the end of the day He is the only person who can help me, who knows all that has happened. He hasn't let me down so far. I don't have to worry. I can trust him to sort it out.

The congregation are singing quietly. It is nearly time for Communion. 'Broken for me, broken for you,' repeats the chorus of the hymn. Pug is upset and has to go out. I bite my lip but carry on. There's a part of me which feels shattered into a million pieces that will never fit together again, but I feel very close to Jesus in my broken state. Some of the letters have compared what I've been through to His persecution. I don't know that I agree theologically, but it has made me more aware of the pain that God must have experienced when He was letting Jesus die for us. The pain of His broken world having gone astray. It is very humbling.

I have asked to have Communion brought to me at the end, when everyone else has been served. I still have to undergo all kinds of tests in case I have picked up an infection, and I don't want to pass anything on to other people. I am not overkeen on the taste of wine and am hoping there will be just a tiny drop left. I should be so lucky. There's loads in the cup. I gulp it down, though I'm not sure how.

Prayers are said for the men. That is not nearly so hard: 'God, get them caught soon, so they can't harm anyone else.' We join in the Lord's Prayer. The words are familiar from childhood days. We had to say them every day in school assembly, a practice I found very boring at the time. Now I miss saying it so regularly. With all the different translations, I flounder to remember the words:

'Forgive us our sins, as we forgive those who sin against us.'

That's straightforward enough, isn't it? Perhaps I don't want to remember? It's too hard-hitting. Can I forgive those men? There's no point in praying the words if I'm not prepared to put them into action. God will know if I mean them, even if no one else does. It doesn't look as if I have a lot of options. I've already discovered from painful experience that if I hold a grudge against someone it is me who suffers. I become bitter and full of resentment.

A family friend made a pass at me one day. I was astounded and very angry. We had known him for years; I had liked and respected him. Just what did he think he was doing? He asked me to forgive him and took me straight home, apologising the whole time. I grunted that I forgave him, and that that would be the end of it. It was not. My lips had moved to make the correct sounds but every time he came near the house I ignored him or was rude.

This went on for about three years, until one day I stopped to think about it. I expected forgiveness that was unconditional, that wiped the slate clean, yet I had gone on hurting this man for years. It was my turn to ask for forgiveness. It was good to be friends again, and to let go of the anger and bitterness. It had done me as much harm as it had him. He had forgotten how it had all begun. After that there never seemed any point in holding a grudge against someone. Life is too short. No one knows what is going to happen next. My views on forgiveness are already sorted out, and fresh in my mind. There is no real problem in praying for the men. I know the consequences of not forgiving others, and do not intend to be destroyed by them a second time.

CHAPTER EIGHT

I do not feel quite so charitably inclined when I see the Sunday papers. The *News of the World* has printed an artist's impression of the events of 6 March. A scantily clad version of me is being dragged from the room at knife-point while Dad and Dave are about to be beaten. My family are furious and it doesn't do David a great deal of good either. By the time I get to the hospital he has managed to get his hands on some newspapers, including the *News of the World*. He is so angry I half expect him to tear it to shreds. The policeman on duty outside the ward resolves the crisis to some extent by removing the papers altogether. Now all I have to do is find something else to keep David occupied. Not an easy task, when the subject at the front of both our minds is the very thing we're not supposed to discuss until he has made his statement.

He has asked for his personal stereo to be brought in but the headphones put too much pressure on his ear. The nurses are doing their best to entertain him, and things are easier now his parents are around, but his father hates hospitals so they haven't stayed long. David still gets confused at times. He's asked me what his mum and dad were doing here. Apparently he remembered to tell his mum about the chocolates, but forgot to mention that they were for her. She ate a few but must have felt guilty that she was eating his sweets. She's left the rest for him.

I visit my dad but he looks as if he is getting worse rather than better. This time we do talk. Not a lot, but enough. He seems to think the press and TV are much more balanced than I do. He is quite impressed with how gentle and caring some of the reporting has been. He wants all the newspaper cuttings for our records, and we are to keep everything we get on video. He's welcome to it. Almost overnight rape has become the hot topic, and looks set to continue that way for some time. I am completely fed up with all the headlines, by-lines, the truth, the whole truth, and everything but the truth.

I know the police have a system where they release so much information to the press in the hope that members of the public will come forward with extra details. I can see the value of that, but I wish there was some way of warning the victim what to expect. The *Daily Mail* has printed its version of the glove worn during the attack. The picture shows a black leather driving glove revealing part of a spider's web tattoo. It is nothing like the actual glove but seeing it has left me feeling very shaken. The police take the line that it will help them. When people ring up and confess to the crime, they will be able to ask what they were wearing. If the reply is a black leather driving glove it rules that person out immediately. That's as maybe. It will be a long time before I can relax when there are black leather driving gloves around.

It's amazing how many people do ring up and waste police time. One woman said she was a medium and the rapists were going to hijack a plane at Luton airport at two in the morning. It all has to be followed up. No wonder there are so many people involved with the case. There are something like two dozen officers investigating all the information. They've had an enormous response to the descriptions and photofits. Members of the criminal underworld have been shopping one another left, right and centre. There have been hundreds of phone calls to the incident centre at Hanwell where everything is being co-ordinated. It should do wonders for their crime clear-up rate if they all get followed up.

My argument is not really with the police. There are very few of them I would find fault with, apart from the doctor. They are doing a superb job and I don't want to hamper them in their work. The thing that bothers me is how everything can be so sensationalised. The press latched on to the story from the beginning and are obviously intent on milking it to the full. Rape always sells papers, and the fact that it happened in a vicarage must be an extra bonus. There's still a sense that it's wrong to defile the house of God, and a vicarage is a sort of extension of that. As for the vicar's daughter being the victim? That has to be good for another few thousand copies. It's interesting to see how they've started to soft-pedal on that piece of information after various people started to shout about anonymity. Now it's more likely to be a 'woman'. Who just happened to be at the Vicarage. Pity no one thought of that before.

The publicity has been a real eye-opener. I assumed that the papers wouldn't be able to write much about me. I understood rape victims had total anonymity. Obviously I was wrong. I'm growing immune to the 'virgin' headlines, but I don't really like them. A lot of people seem to think they're a complete fabrication; kind of 'They had to say that, didn't they, with her being the vicar's daughter'. I guess that kind of person wouldn't be convinced even if I showed them the blood on the sheet.

Some of the stories the papers have come up with have been fascinating, especially the ones about my courage. I didn't feel courageous. I just did what I thought I should. The way the press are building me up makes me feel as if I'm reading about a different person. There are so many inaccuracies too. According to one paper David is a Sunday-school teacher. He would say he is an agnostic. Someone else has us as engaged, which is a bit premature to say the least. Our ages are a constant source of amusement. One day we will be twenty-five, the next twenty. It's even been known for them to change within a few lines in the same paper.

What is not so amusing is the fact that practically every paper has reported that Dad and David saw me raped. They did not. I wish I could write it in letters a foot high across every news hoarding in the land. I accept that the story is news and people want to print it. What I can't handle is the amount they want to write, and the things they invent when they can't get proper information. The rape was bad enough. This is like a second violation. I have no control over anything that is happening. It frustrates me that there is no way of setting the record straight. We're sticking to police advice and saying nothing, despite the pressures. The press are doing their best to get interviews. Every opportunity they have, they grab. They're like leeches sucking for blood. Would I talk to this one or that one? They will give me so much for an exclusive.

Rachel has actually rung one paper and asked them to leave us alone. It's quite true that a lot of what is written is made up, particularly the so-called 'quotes'. We have consistently made only one response to the press: 'Get lost.' Or rather the police version, which sounds a bit more polite. Dad is a law unto himself. He's handling his own affairs as far as reporters are concerned. He's got more experience than I have.

I have a horrible feeling that it's only a matter of time before someone goes the whole hog and prints my photo in the paper. From day one they have been tripping over one another to get a picture. The police are doing their best to prevent it but I refuse to stay locked indoors, or go grovelling around under a blanket any more. I do what I can to confuse the photographers, like wearing a jumper with Pug's name on when we went to church. The rest I have to leave to common human decency.

It is a misplaced trust. Monday morning arrives, along with a full-length photograph of me on the front page of the *Sun*. My face and the name on the jumper have been blacked out, otherwise there I am for the world to see. Joe is on the phone at the first opportunity. This kind of thing cannot continue. He contacts the Press Council. They assure him that they are already launching their own investigation into media activity surrounding the case.

It is some consolation. Meanwhile all we can do is get on with living. I haven't been to see David yet today. It's good to be on the move. At Charing Cross Hospital Rachel has problems finding a parking space. I rejoice in the unexpected freedom of going ahead in the lift on my own. My joy is short-lived. As I stand waiting for the lift to arrive I suddenly realise that I am wearing the same skirt, boots and jacket that are splashed across the front page of the *Sun*. I feel as if everyone is looking at me. How could I be so stupid? Fancy coming out in the same clothes whilst copies of the paper are all over the place? Everyone will know who I am and what I've been through. They should not have that access to me. It hurts.

Despite the cries of outrage over the existing coverage the TV people want to know if I will do an interview for them if I am blacked out. They believe it will help to find the men. I very much doubt it. Anyway what is the point in trying to protect my identity? To all intents and purposes everyone knows it.

When I recover enough of my shattered self-esteem I write to Harry Greenway, a local MP and a family friend, who has been making the right kind of noises on our behalf. He has already been to visit my father in hospital and has expressed outrage in Parliament about the way the law stands at present. The whole affair certainly seems to be stirring up a hornet's nest. MPs, lawyers, journalists (of the more respectable variety), members of the public, and the National Council for Civil Liberty are all hollering for a change in the law – especially when the Attorney General issues a statement to the effect that the *Sun* has committed no offence by publishing my photograph. The Act that prohibits identification only applies after a person is accused of rape. It appears that my whole life story can be printed right up until the time somebody is arrested, as long as it helps the case. The police may ask the press to go easy but there aren't very strict rules about it – apart from the ones protecting the men involved. It all seems so unjust. I become headline news. The rapist's identity appears to be secure until he is found guilty. I am speechless. Fortunately Harry Greenway isn't. He leads a group of MPs in the tabling of a Commons motion requesting that legislation should be introduced 'as a matter of urgency to prohibit absolutely the publishing of the name or identity of any alleged rape victim by direct or indirect means'.

I have found my voice. Amen to that.

CHAPTER NINE

My cough and cold are getting worse. So is the pain in my ribs. Rachel rings the GP. She calls to see me after morning surgery. I still have blood coming from my hymen so she examines me internally. She assures me that it will stop soon, but is very concerned about my chest and throat. She thinks I may be on the verge of bronchitis. Unfortunately she is hesitant to prescribe any drugs to ease the pain as the police have arranged an appointment at the special clinic in two days' time, and drugs could affect the tests.

What she can offer me is the 'morning-after' pill. My mind is in a whirl. Could I be pregnant? When we discussed abortion at CYFA camp in my teens I was assured by a medical student that pregnancy as the result of rape was very rare. How rare? Did the rapist manage to ejaculate sperm into me? How can you tell? What if I am carrying his child? I've never been in favour of abortion, including the IUD and the morning-after pill. Should I compromise in this situation? The doctor is waiting for an answer. It is the last chance I will have for the pill to be effective. I decline the offer.

To take my mind off the new, disturbing possibilities I go for a walk with Mum and Pug. It is the first time I have been out on the streets, apart from the few yards to the YMCA, and I still feel that everyone is looking at me. I am beginning to wonder if I have two heads or some dreaded plague. I am due to go to the sheltered housing complex for the monthly service in the evening. I want to see Mrs Richmond and tell her that I am all right, but I don't know if I can face being on display again. No one will know what to say to me. I think people are afraid to mention what has happened. They don't realise that I'm not frightened of talking about it. On the contrary, I find it very hard to talk about anything else. In the end Jim comes with me to the home. That will confuse everyone. They've seen me with several different men over the last few months. At least it will give them a new topic of conversation. Mrs Richmond is sitting in the lounge with the others, waiting for the service to begin. Her eyes glaze with tears when she sees me. She takes hold of my hand and does not let go. She holds it all through the service, giving it an extra squeeze when things get a bit close for comfort. Before we leave she gives me a hug. She is so relieved to know that I am OK.

I wish the same could be said for everyone else. Wednesday brings the usual mountain of mail. Amongst the good wishes is a letter of a very different nature. With no signature. It isn't the first of its kind to arrive but this one is addressed to me. The person who wrote it has obviously seen my photograph on the front page of the papers and does not approve. He complains that I should have stayed in my house on Sunday where no one could have seen me, and kept away from everyone. How dare I go to church? It will be the only time in my life that anyone will want to photograph me, or see my stupid face. I am referred to as a 'silly bitch' and a 'stupid cow'. the same kind of pleasant language the rapist used. The postscript is particularly upsetting:

'I will be keeping my eye on you.'

I read the words, but cannot believe I am seeing them. I am shaking with anger. I didn't ask the press to take photographs of me, and I'm certainly not going to stay imprisoned in the very place I was attacked just to suit this man's whims. I read the letter out to the people in the room, then tear it into tiny pieces. The only positive thing about it is that the stamp can go with the others to the Royal National Lifeboat Institution.

I know Dad has been receiving mail in a similar vein. I have only seen a few of the letters, but it is immediately obvious which paper the senders have been reading by the questions they ask. Did the dirty old man enjoy the sight? Did it give him a kick? There are so many distortions of the truth. I know these people are misinformed and ill but it just makes me want to cry out about the sick nature of it all, including the chauvinistic view that women are created for cooking and sex; nothing else.

The police tell me later that the senders could have been prosecuted for sending offensive mail, but by then the letters are at the bottom of the dustbin covered in rubbish and finger-prints. If we had known earlier we would have been more careful. Apparently the police can take prints from a piece of paper for up to three months.

At the time I am in such a state I am hardly capable of rational thinking. I don't think I have ever been so angry. Haven't I been through enough? It's bad not being allowed out on my own. Everywhere I go I have to have a chaperone: Jim; the police; Rachel. I grumble about my restricted freedom but am not given any option. I am due to sign on, but I'm not even allowed to go to the unemployment benefit office, in case I meet one of the men. A police officer goes for me. I need to know if the rape will affect my claim in any way. The police are given a purple form: 'To be filled in only in the event of pregnancy as a result of rape.' I am not over-impressed with the subtlety of the DHSS. The rape happened six days ago, not six weeks. Even if it feels like it at times.

I've had to give myself a severe talking to. Every time the heating goes on in the Vicarage the joints creak and frighten the life out of me. It sounds as though people are walking about upstairs. I must ignore the noises or I am going to turn into jelly. The squeaky boards are nothing new. They have always been the same.

Pug panics more than I do. She ground an entire tube to a halt one day. She saw someone in a carriage she thought fitted one of the descriptions, so she got off at Hammersmith and ran and told the guard. The guard shut the doors and Pug had to go through all the carriages with a policeman. When they found the man she suspected he was taken off for questioning. Pug was really embarrassed because it held up the train for quite a long time.

Apparently the WPC has had a long chat with her about what happened last week. I didn't want Pug to know, in case it hurt her, but her mind has been running riot without any proper information to work on. I certainly don't want her building an impression from what the papers have to say. They are making everyone feel worse.

Thursday brings a new flurry of activity. A week has passed and the police are out with a mobile incident unit. The cadets from Hendon are combing the allotments. The police already know that the men went down the alleyway at the side of the house because someone has produced the cricket bat from a garden. Now they are looking for further clues.

Mum is kept on the move making hot drinks. I watch impassively. I still haven't cried. Maybe I will with Dave. He's had so little involvement; perhaps being there if and when I cry could be his contribution. When at last we are alone I tell him briefly what happened. It is far from easy and Dave obviously finds it as difficult as I do. A solitary tear trickles down his cheek. It means more than a fountain full. My eyes are still dry. Perhaps it's just as well. I have a friend's funeral to face afterwards. Just to help things along.

Mum takes a break to visit Dad. She has been going every day. I go when I have to. I still can't relate to him somehow. The swelling in his eye looks revolting. His condition deteriorated to such an extent that at one point they considered transferring him to Charing Cross. He couldn't take his food and was being sick all the time, which burnt his oesophagus. We think he must have come off the drip too soon for his body to be able to cope.

He's on the mend now, though, and has done an interview for television. The papers do not miss such a golden opportunity. He is back in the headlines: 'The forgiving vicar'; 'I feel no hate for men'; 'Attacked vicar feels no hatred'. Some people seem surprised by his attitude and imply that he has no right to forgive the men. If that is the case, why did Jesus leave such clear guidelines in the Lord's Prayer? Perhaps they don't know it? They never had to learn it at junior school?

People don't need to concern themselves about what I think. For once I agree with Dad. I've already forgiven the men. The only comment of his I object to is the one about me being 'the jewel in his crown'. I find that very embarrassing. It's not like him. I've never really heard him express much emotion. Why should he single out me, and not Pug or Rachel? I don't deserve it. If I had to describe myself it would more likely be as a rough diamond.

Dad reckons he used the phrase because he wanted to relate it to something people would think about, and everyone has been watching the TV series *The Jewel in the Crown*. I think that's a load of rubbish. I'm not into gemstones and valuable jewellery. They don't mean anything to me. I don't even like gold. If I wear jewellery it's usually silver, and likely to stay that way since the robbery.

The papers are full of the fact that the police are holding several suspects, but I'm not going to build up any hopes. There's already been one false lead over the weekend and I know just how accurate the papers can be. I will concentrate on the next hurdle. It's big enough.

Nine days ago I was a virgin. Now I am off to visit a venereal disease clinic. The police have made the arrangements and to my relief two of the policewomen are coming with me. The clinic is part of a normal hospital, not far away, on the edge of Acton. It's only a small building cut off from the main block but immediately I mention the name everyone seems to know what it is. The atmosphere is relaxed, the receptionist friendly, but while I am sitting in the waiting room I can't help looking round and wondering why everyone else is there. I guess a lot of people are receiving treatment for thrush and things like that, but there's no way I would attend a clinic if I had the choice. Going to my own GP is embarrassing enough. Suddenly it strikes me that the others are probably wondering even worse things about us. Why would three women, one middle-aged and two fairly young, all come to such a place together?

The policewomen seem to sense the unspoken questions. One speaks to a nurse and we are ushered into a separate room. I don't know if it is better or worse. Now there is nothing to think about, other than the impending examination. I make a joke of it, but underneath I hate being here. There are lots of leaflets around explaining all about the different sexually transmitted diseases people can catch. I don't want to know. We had to study them at college and for Biology O level. That was more than enough.

The doctor is a specialist in the area of rape. Number two in the country, so I am informed. When we first meet her attitude is a bit brusque and my heart sinks. What if I don't get on with her very well? I don't think I could stand it a second time round. She talks to us briefly, then takes me to her consulting room to ask more questions. Have I been on the pill? Used any contraceptives? Am I a smoker? Are there any hereditary ill-nesses in the family? Can I take all types of medicine? Do I have any allergies? Have I had any operations? The questions cover a wide area, and give her a brief outline of my medical history and social behaviour. I need not have worried. Now that we are talking she is kindness itself.

She has to examine me, but she takes far more care than the police doctor. I won't say having swabs taken from the vagina, anus, urethra and throat are pleasant experiences, and I don't want them repeated in a hurry, but she does things smoothly and efficiently. Much to my surprise, there isn't even any hassle with the blood tests. Doctors usually have to have several goes before they manage to get my blood. This one hits first time.

The tests will show if any signs of infection are already presenting themselves. They will let me have the results in about ten days, although gonorrhoea can take up to four weeks to be diagnosed, and syphilis three months. More tests will be necessary in the future. The doctor is matter-of-fact, but caring. It might almost be reassuring, if we weren't talking about such horrifying possibilities. At least I won't have to worry about arranging a pregnancy test. I presume they have done one.

Going home in the car Carol, the WDI, senses how down I am feeling. She emphasises again that the team are all 'on call' if I need them and mentions other agencies like the Rape Crisis Centre. She explains how I can bury the whole thing dead by working through the pain and trauma and leaving them behind. Or I can bury it alive. That means closing my mind to the pain, pretending that it isn't there. And living with the consequences. I know my choice. With people like Carol to back me I know I can win. I am not going to let those men destroy me. I will bury it dead.

CHAPTER TEN

The men have been arrested and are being charged. I can feel safe again. The police have certainly not wasted any time. My trust in them has not been misplaced. They are equally impressed by the response of the public. They've had over a thousand phone calls during the past week.

We have picked up various bits and pieces, although obviously the police haven't been able to tell us much. I think they've been surprised how many things I've worked out for myself. They reckon I should have been a detective because I'm quite good at getting the different bits of information and piecing them all together. I think I'm just plain nosy. I also like an excuse to chat to them. Some of them aren't bad-looking. We've seen the whole team far more than I expected. In lots of ways they have become almost like members of the family.

I hate to admit it, but they were probably right to keep me from wandering around locally too much. It looks as though none of the men who have been arrested come from a million miles away. Now that they are safely under lock and key I am actually being allowed up to the shops in Ealing, as long as I am accompanied. I have a special task to perform and time is running out. Someone has given the family a big white teddy bear called Everest. Both my sisters have fallen in love with him and refuse to be parted from him, which is causing something of a problem as Rachel will be going back to her own home soon.

The only answer is to buy another. It is not as simple as it sounds. He is not the easiest of bears to come across. Or the cheapest. None of the local toy shops have one in stock, so we end up ordering one. He is to be called Snowdon. It's quite appropriate considering the steepness of his price. We are continually amazed by how generous people have been in the things they have given us.

Dad is taking up the offer of someone's home for a holiday as soon as he feels up to it. He and David are being discharged from hospital today, which is something of a miracle considering the state they were both in and the fact that it's only eight days since the attack. At one stage David had a blood clot on the brain which they thought might need an operation, to add to his other injuries. Dad has lost a lot of weight, but his speech is less slurred, and the black eye is fading. Thank heavens.

He arrives home on the regular ambulance service with the reporters once more in pursuit. This time they don't want to know about me. I have to keep out of the way so that I don't ruin their shots. All they are interested in is the arrest. I am not expecting to be cold-shouldered and find it nearly as difficult to handle as the earlier publicity. One minute I am the centre of attention, the next I'm being asked to move to one side or they won't be able to use the film. It's a bit like the mother and baby syndrome we learnt about at college. Mum gets all the attention whilst she is pregnant, but as soon as the baby comes along it becomes the focus of attention and mum gets left out. I know how she must feel. All empty and neglected. The press have built me up to be something special. Now that it has stopped I fall to earth with a bang.

Dad has informed the reporters that he will be going away for a holiday. He needs time to relax and recover. I won't argue with that. I am badly in need of a break myself. I have lost half a stone in weight and am still experiencing a lot of pain in my ribs. If David is fit enough we hope to go up to Scotland with his parents on Monday.

He is staying with friends, rather than at the YMCA. He will be quieter there. His mum and dad have stayed down all week and been fantastic, especially considering his dad's hatred of hospitals. They've spent hours visiting David, and have kept him well supplied with food. He didn't think much of hospital catering. Now his grandmother is down for the weekend, helping to look after him. I go to see him as soon as I can. He is wearing a hat with a fluffy inside to keep his ears warm, and has been asleep for most of the time since he came out of hospital. He looks far from well so I don't stay long.

By Saturday afternoon David is ready to take on the world. Or thinks he is. He is convinced he can make it to Ealing Broadway to do some shopping. We try to dissuade him, but he is determined. Eventually he compromises. He will go to the shops at the end of the road. He makes it there, but I more or less have to drag him back draped around my shoulders. It's a slow journey, with frequent pauses for breath, and by the time we get back to the house both of us are exhausted. He admits he is not as strong as he thought he was and promises to take things a bit slower.

Sunday is a little quieter. There are a few reporters hanging around, but not many. In church a lady I don't know asks if her little girl can give me a kiss. She thinks I have been so brave. It's not exactly easy over the back of the pew, but that hug and kiss mean the world to me. I make a quick exit after the service. I don't think I can handle a mass of people all wanting to know how I am. Dad is going away in the afternoon so it is a good excuse to go home for lunch.

First thing Monday morning David does a disappearing act. He has gone out for a walk on his own and no one knows where he is. When he hasn't returned after a couple of hours we are all beginning to have visions of him in a state of collapse somewhere. I do what I can to help but my GP wants to check my breathing and the condition of my ribs because I am still in so much pain. She decides I must go to the local hospital for an

X-ray before I go anywhere. Great. If Dave has collapsed, that could mean two of us ending up in casualty.

Rachel has gone home. Mum and Pug are back at work. I am alone in the house. So far it has not worried me unduly. Now it presents a major problem: no transport. The GP is already running late for her next clinic but there is no way she is going to let me struggle up to the X-ray department alone. She threatens to drive me there herself if no one else is available. Maybe someone from the YMCA will run me up there? She drives me round to the YMCA and waits till a lift is confirmed before she will leave me.

David is not at the hospital, at least not in the part where I have to wait. Perhaps he has returned home by now. His mum will be going spare if he is still missing. Thankfully I do not have to wait too long worrying about him. The radiographer calls me in and gives me something else to think about instead. She wants to know if I am pregnant. That's a good question. I say no, and pray I'm correct.

The GP rings with the results of the X-ray later in the afternoon. There is nothing broken, which has been her main concern. Perhaps I pulled a muscle when I turned sharply in the car in Scotland? She still cannot prescribe drugs as I have to have more tests at the special clinic, but she hopes I have a nice holiday. David has eventually turned up safe and sound. We might make it to Scotland after all. He had been shopping in Ealing Broadway and lost track of the time.

It's not long before we are due at Euston to catch the overnight train so it's all systems go. The journey is long, cold and not very comfortable. The previous night the train had been too hot so to average things out the heating has been switched off completely. I can't sleep because whichever way I turn my ribs hurt. Watching a video might help to pass the time but the video has been stolen. We are left with nothing to do but doze fitfully and stare into the darkness. We are all relieved when we arrive in Glasgow. Kenny, the friend with the car, is coming to meet us. We will be indoors soon. Unfortunately even that does not go according to plan. Kenny has been held up in Glasgow's rush hour, and we have to stand in a cold station waiting for him.

When we arrive in Cumbernauld all we want to do is get warm and go to sleep. I understood Cumbernauld only had two distinctive features: the fact that it has no traffic lights, and that it's the place where *Gregory's Girl* was filmed. I've found out since my last visit that there's more to the town than meets the eye. There's quite a big tax office, so a lot of income tax forms come up here. Apparently they're the main employer. I don't know if that's another claim to fame, or one they would rather keep quiet about. All that concerns me is that hardly anybody here has connected David and me with the events in the papers. Cumbernauld is a fairly big new town and London is a long way away. It's good to feel we can walk down the street without people staring. There are no phones ringing or doorbells going. We can relax and sleep all day if we wish.

By Wednesday David and his dad are raring to go again. They have decided we should see a bit of Scotland. We take some sausages, a camping stove, a shotgun and Ace, the dog. David's mum looks sceptical when she hears the men talking about a short trip. It usually ends up as an overnight stay according to her. By the time we get to Fort William it's obvious that her prediction was right. I am not worried either way. Scotland is beautiful. I am content to relax and enjoy the scenery. Stirling, Ben Nevis, Loch Ness. We look vaguely for signs of a monster, but there are none in evidence. It's perhaps just as well as David takes his dad's gun and starts firing into the lake for target practice. The lake is big enough, so he can hardly miss, but I'm worried about his ears. His dad is licensed to own a gun and they go out shooting crows and things, but when we have been out on other occasions David has usually worn earmuffs. This time he had nothing to protect his ears. The doctors would not be happy if they knew. Ace thinks it is all enormous fun, and tries his hardest to get down to the water for a swim. It is still very cold and none of us fancy a wet dog in the car so we keep feeding him sausages to stop him straying.

David is less easily distracted. When we are back in the car he wants a turn driving. His dad is not so keen. He reminds David he was warned at the hospital not to drive; they have been pumping so many drugs into him. David argues, but has to give in eventually. It must be very frustrating for him.

One thing we do all agree on is the fact that we must find somewhere to stay overnight soon. We drive round Inverness but there is nowhere cheap enough, or with the right number of rooms. Not many places are geared to the tourist trade in March and the one big hotel is far too expensive. Dave's dad drives on. I am just beginning to wonder if we are going to have to sleep in the car when we find a bed and breakfast in a small village about seven miles from Aviemore. To everyone's relief it has the number of rooms required and is relatively cheap. We are not going to have to freeze to death in the car.

Neither are we going to starve. There is a restaurant down the street. David orders haggis. I taste a bit but won't be in a hurry to try it again. The family seem to think it highly amusing. Altogether it's a very pleasant evening. I'm glad I met David's parents before 6 March. It's good to be with them, away from all the pressures.

When we get back to the bed and breakfast they are ready for bed. David and I work on a different time mechanism and have no intention of sleeping yet. We go into the lounge and sit talking quietly. David has been very supportive and it seems natural to tell him my worries. I have only known him two and a half months, and most of that time has been pretty traumatic, but in some ways the events of the last couple of weeks have brought us closer than we were before. He was there. He knows what it felt like. I can share things with him on a level that is not possible with other people. Including my most pressing concern of the moment: Am I pregnant?

Someone comes in and switches off the light but when they realise we are still in the room they switch it back on again. If they are hinting it is time to go to bed we aren't taking any notice. There are no nurses, no visitors, no police officers, no time limits. Just us and the flickering fire. Suddenly the peace is shattered. David is asking the question I thought no man would ever want to ask me after what has happened. Will I marry him?

CHAPTER ELEVEN

I am shocked, flattered, amazed. I may feel soiled and second-hand, but David still wants me. Last night he offered me all I really want, but how can I give him any kind of realistic reply? So many thoughts are racing through my mind. I don't even know the name of the village where we are staying, let alone the answer to such a tempting proposition. My emotions are in a turmoil. We both need some kind of stability, the knowledge that the other is going to be around, but I don't know that an engagement is right. Not yet, anyway. We have known each other for such a short time. Events have made us both very vulnerable.

The police have told me to consider myself still a virgin. They reckon what happened had nothing to do with my choice. That's fine in theory, not quite so easy to put into practice when I am becoming increasingly uneasy that I could be pregnant. I will not consider such a possibility. My period is often late. I have had nothing but trouble with menstruation from the word go. I will concentrate on eating. A full English breakfast takes some concentration, even with the dog helping me out by eating a couple of sausages.

Sitting in the car watching the scenery roll past is less demanding. Aviemore, Aberdeen, Arbroath, Dundee. Like the breakfast, there is quite a lot of it. Despite the distractions of oil rigs, and hundred-mile-an-hour crosswinds along the coastal road, there is too much time for thinking. I feel sick, tired, scared. It is quite a small car and when we drive through an exposed part I can feel it being shaken around. It doesn't help much when we go past several lorries that have been blown over. I don't know which is worse, the buffeting we are getting from the wind, or the pounding in my own brain.

Did they do a pregnancy test at the hospital? If I am pregnant what will I do? I have always wanted to be a mum. Could I carry a child, and then give it up? On the other hand, if I keep it could I love it knowing how it was conceived? Could I cope with the constant reminders, or the dreadful task of answering the inevitable questions about its father? There would be times when I would be sure to look at that child with hatred. Even if the child was adopted it could trace me in eighteen, twenty years' time, wanting to know why it had been given away. The adoptive parents would face the same kind of dilemma. How do you tell someone, 'Sorry, you were the result of a rape'? How can anyone live with that kind of knowledge? It would destroy me. Is it fair to impose it on anyone else? Maybe I would miscarry? With our family history it could be a distinct possibility. Would that solve the problem, or create more? Then I would be constantly worrying whether I could ever carry a child. Abortion might be the answer, if I agreed with it. I've always thought anyone who was stupid enough to get themselves pregnant should be responsible for the consequences. Must I reconsider my views? Could I live with myself knowing that I had killed something God had created, even as a consequence of rape? I know women do suffer after abortions. I am sure I would be no exception.

My head is still spinning with questions when we pause for a break in Dundee. In my agitation I manage to drop David's eardrops in the middle of the high street. I feel terrible when we go into the chemist and discover they can only be bought on prescription. David doesn't seem to think it is too drastic. He doesn't like having them in the first place, and reckons he can get some more from the doctor in Cumbernauld. I'll believe it when I see him using them.

Eventually we arrive back at his parents' house and decide to go and visit Kenny and his sister. We play Trivial Pursuit but I am so tired I can hardly keep my eyes open. We have been up from the crack of dawn till gone midnight. It has been a rough day. In all senses of the word. I have had enough. Someone can wake me when it's all over.

The next morning there is still no sign to tell me I can stop worrying about pregnancy. Nor the next. My period is now a week late and I am getting very concerned. David and I have travelled down to Birmingham for a planning weekend for the holiday mission I help with in Wales. It is hard to concentrate on the discussions with such a big question mark hanging over my own future but I do my best. People express surprise that I've made it to the meetings, but they are glad to see that I look all right. By the end of the day several friends are aware how deceptive appearances can be as I open up the worry and hurt and ask them to pray about it. Someone suggests if I had a scrape it might sort out my other problems and I need never know whether I was pregnant or not. They can go and jump. It would still be an abortion, whatever name it was given. Besides, I don't think for one moment the doctors would accept the idea.

I am woken at six on Sunday morning by the girl I am sharing a room with going to the loo. Her period has started. Two hours later I follow suit. I want to wake up the whole house and dance around shouting and singing, only I don't think they would appreciate it. Instead I crawl back to bed for a couple of hours. As I snuggle under the bedclothes it feels so good to be free of that nagging anxiety, to know that I no longer have to worry about the terrible choices, even if I am experiencing the usual stomach cramps and feeling generally under-the-weather.

As soon as I see Dave I tell him I am not pregnant. He has

only just woken up and wants to know if I have had a test. He is in good company. The men all ask how I know. I cannot believe that intelligent males, two of them with degrees, are still unable to put two and two together. Do they really think I would find out the results from a doctor first thing on a Sunday morning miles away from home?

Monday is a different matter. I am on the phone to the special clinic at the first opportunity. I have been given a number to use instead of my name, and I quote it conscientiously. The sister at the other end immediately knows who I am and greets me like a long-lost friend. She puts me through to the doctor. Most of the tests are negative, but they want me down at the clinic to give me treatment for an anal infection. It's nothing to worry about. It will clear up with tablets in a week or so. As soon as I reach the hospital I tell them I am not pregnant. They are very relieved. It was too early to do a test; they were hoping I would tell them as soon as I knew. It's always a big anxiety. The medical student was wrong; it's a dangerous myth that a woman cannot become pregnant from rape.

My relief is tinged with sadness. Although I have told everyone I am not pregnant I know there are cases where periods have continued throughout pregnancy. Maybe I will be one of those? I am horrified to find myself entertaining such a possibility. What would the doctor think if she knew how my mind was working? How could part of me still wish I was pregnant after all the questions that have been whirling round my head?

The doctor is trying to warn me about possible side effects from the treatment for the infection. I don't want to know. I have not got any major disease. I have got off lightly. My records will only be kept for a year. If I had syphilis they would keep them for ten. I wonder fleetingly what happens if someone has AIDS. The whole thing sounds horrifying from what I have occasionally heard mentioned in the media.

It would be interesting to know how the rapist has fared. If he has had to go through similar tests. I had thrush when he attacked me. I don't want to be malicious, but if he has caught an infection from me, it would balance things up a bit.

CHAPTER TWELVE

Almost before I have time to get my breath back it is Easter. I have never thought of it in terms of Easter eggs and pretty flowers. It has always been a time to think of Jesus dying. I can't remember ever not knowing that He died for the sins of the whole world, although I find it much harder to acknowledge that that includes me. I don't like to think of all that suffering specifically for me. Death is painful. Pete's death taught me that. This Easter I am even more conscious of the fact. Somehow I feel a lot closer to God. I can understand more of the pain He must have gone through letting Jesus die, and letting the rape happen to me. In a sense it's as if He is saying, 'I'm going to let you share this pain, so Jesus's death will be far more relevant to you.'

It's the same with the Resurrection. I have looked straight at death. When life was given back to me I realised just how precious it is. The only problem is I get so impatient with other people's worries and concerns. They seem so insignificant after staring death in the face. When people are fretting about trivia I want to say 'Don't worry about that. It's not worth it. It won't do you any good.' I'm having to relearn how to be sensitive to other people's concerns, but it's not easy. I am really frustrated seeing people so wrapped up in their tiny little world, getting bogged down by minor problems. Life's too short.

Because I have seen God bring me through such a major event it's helped me to trust him far more with the small things. I simply say 'OK, God, I've got a problem here. Can you do something about it?' and let him get on with it. I've always been a great believer in arrow prayers. Short and to the point. Now they are part and parcel of everyday life.

They often include the men as their targets. I try to encourage others to pray for them, but it's hard going. If I am at a Christian meeting and I ask people to pray for the men very few respond. Someone made the excuse that people don't know what to say. What makes them think that I do? All I know is they are still people, whatever they have done. They are in custody. The prison gates have shut behind them. I know that the prison fraternity hates rapists. Prisoners like to think that their wives and children are safe in the outside world. If a rapist comes in, or a child molester, they may themselves be raped unless they are segregated for their own good. Those men need all the prayer they can get.

I go to a reunion at my old school. Reactions are very interesting. A few of the girls haven't connected events with us at all; some obviously know but are just skating round it. Others aren't sure whether it was Pug or me involved. In the end I put them out of their misery by broaching the subject and we just carry on from there. All the barriers are down. We can talk freely.

When people will listen, I am more than ready to talk. They get the whole lot. They don't have to worry about never having dealt with the situation before, or about finding something spectacular to say. I don't know what is expected any more than they do. I'm certainly not going to come up with any flashy answers.

Sometimes it becomes quite laughable. Because I talk freely with people who are really concerned I often find people who overhear bits of the conversation trying to eavesdrop without appearing to do so. I nearly got up to invite someone over to our table once. He was edging closer and closer. I was afraid he was going to do his back in.

I have to be sensitive to how much people can take, but it's good to be able to talk. Especially when I can see it helping others. It means I get all the tales of woe, but somehow there's a strength in sharing at a level people wouldn't normally consider. One friend came to pour out his anxieties and went away saying, 'Talking to you really puts my problems into perspective.'

At the other extreme, I do come across people who treat me as though I had horns. Just like they do when someone has died, they will cross the road or scuttle to another section of the shop. They don't know how to handle it so they get out of the way. The ones I find hardest are the people who talk to me as though it hasn't happened. How can you ignore something like that? I'd like to at times, but there are too many reminders.

At the moment the police are recommending that we apply for Criminal Injuries, a compensation scheme for victims of violent crime. We can't claim until after the court case, but they want to make sure we have the necessary details. Part of me wants nothing to do with it. It smacks too much of blood money. On the other hand it is my blood that has been spilt. The medics can do heart transplants, the lot. They can't replace what I have lost. In some ways I have become very cynical. We've just had a leaflet for Neighbourhood Watch pushed through our door. I have one response: 'A bit late, isn't it?'

It's the same with self-defence. I've never really considered a proper course. I'm too much of a coward; I couldn't handle being thrown around, inflicting pain on myself readily and willingly. I've read what I could on the subject, though, especially after the incident in Walpole Park. I know a woman should walk fast and confidently, holding her head up. If she is wearing stilettos she should go for the kneecap. Otherwise, aim for the eyes or the testicles. She might be sued for it; at least she'll be alive to argue the case. But it isn't always just one man. Nobody ever warned me that there could be more than one, or that my attackers might be armed. What use is self-defence against weapons? When it came to the crunch I used the only method I could think of. I tried to get rid of the knife. Other than that there was not a lot I could do.

It's taken time, but I am actually being allowed out on my own now. It's a bit like growing up all over again, being fourteen and allowed up to the shops by myself for the first time. It's a weird sensation. Streets during the day don't bother me, and I quite enjoy walking in the dark on my own. There's a rebellious streak in me that's saying, 'You can't get to me. I'm not going to let you. Nothing else can happen that's bad.' Otherwise I'll end up a bundle of nerves. I won't ever be able to go out on my own, and there are times when I'm going to need to, for my own independence and survival. It's no use relying on anyone else.

It's ironic really. There's a song in the charts with a couple of lines about a man being a hero, fighting for his woman's honour. The song is brilliant, but I find those lines difficult to take. Where were the two men who could have provided that role when I needed them? They weren't heroes. They didn't fight for my honour. My image of men has been shattered. I have a nasty feeling it will take a long time to rebuild.

CHAPTER THIRTEEN

It is Monday 14 April, five weeks since the attack, and the day set for the identification parades. The men are being held in separate places so we have to go to three different police stations. The first is the local one at Ealing, but we have to be there early, before the police start to gather in people for the line-up. The police collect us in a car and on arrival usher us into a waiting room. I am very apprehensive. I have never done anything like this before and don't know quite what to expect. Other than the fact that I will have to see those men again. Police come and go. Time drags on. One hour . . . Two. I have eaten very little and feel slightly sick. Whether it's from hunger or fear, I wouldn't like to say.

We have no idea which man will be first, although the police want to know if the balaclava they have available is like the one worn during the attack. It isn't really but apparently we can ask for the men in the line-up to put it on, or speak, if we think it will help. Does that mean this could be Man 1? If so I don't think he will need to wear a balaclava for me to recognise him. There was something unusual about his eyes.

If only they would get on with it. A lot of the instructions go straight over my head I am so wound up about the whole thing. At last they are ready. Dad has to go first. Then David. I am so nervous that when my turn finally comes they almost push me into the identification room. I am expecting a glass partition with the men at a safe distance behind it. Instead I find myself in a tiny room with a horseshow of men in light blue boiler suits only a matter of inches away from me. I am asked if I understand the procedure but can barely grunt a reply. I had never imagined the men would be so close. My legs are like jelly, and I want to be sick.

As I walk slowly along the line I am convinced that one of them looks vaguely like Man 2. Was I wrong about the line-up being to identify Man 1? I forget all about balaclavas and voice identification. Their nearness and the blue boiler suits have thrown me completely. I have been expecting them to be wearing ordinary clothes. Something that would give me a clue. Why didn't the police warn me it would be like this? As we near the end of the line one of the men blinks. There is nothing significant in that, apart from the fact that it lasts fractionally too long. I am unable to see his eyes properly. Is it deliberate? Could it be Man 1 after all? I am asked if I could positively identify anyone. I shake my head. Even if I could I doubt very much if I could speak in front of them. All I want to do is get out of the room as quickly as possible.

Back upstairs the police explain that the boiler suits are used to prevent people being distinguished by background or status. They try to reassure me that I need not have worried about being so close. If the man had lifted one finger the others would have lynched him. That's not the point. It's being in the same room as one of them that's bugging me, even if it was the one who did least damage to me personally. I have not been able to give a positive identification but my hunch is correct. The blink is significant.

Does it confirm my belief that this man set out to commit a burglary and was horrified by what later took place? During the raid he smashed a picture of me. Was it because he couldn't bear to look at it, knowing what the others were doing? I shall probably never know the reasons behind what happened, but I feel sure this man has a conscience about it.

Being unable to identify him positively has not helped my confidence, though. I thought that if I could identify any of them it would be him. Man 2 will be next if they are in order. My stomach heaves again. I warn the police that I feel sick. One of the men from CID suggests it might be a good idea to have something to eat. Then at least I will have something inside me and my body can decide whether it is a false alarm or not.

That sounds reasonable. There is an hour to spare so we go home for lunch. I pick up my knitting before we are hauled off to Acton. If we are in for another long wait at least I will have something to do. It seems a good idea but I find it is impossible to concentrate. We can't discuss the case. We can't go anywhere in case we bump into one of the people they are lining up for the parade. All I can do is sit looking out of the windows, wondering how much longer it is going to be. Police come and go. It is taking a long time to get people in off the streets. Being part of an identification parade is not a popular pastime and after more than an hour the police only have seven people. When they do finally have enough for a line-up the man's solicitor objects because they don't look sufficiently like his client. There is a possibility it could go to a confrontation, but in the end the whole thing is postponed. I am convinced now that this has to be for Man 2.

We have spent a large chunk of the day hanging around, but there is still a third man to identify at West Drayton Police Station. This is to be a straight confrontation. Only one man will be in the room, apart from the solicitors and police. All I have to say is 'Yes' or 'No'. I ask for the man to have his hands in front of him. Man 3 was the one with the letters tattooed on his fingers, not Man 1 as I first thought. When I see the tattoos I will recognise them instantly.

The police have finished telling us what to expect. It is time for the confrontation. I am to be first this time. I feel weak at the knees again and ask for someone to hold on to me in case I collapse. The room we enter is at least four times as large as the first one. The man is standing at the far end. He looks young, pale, and sheepish. His hair looks different but I have no problem recognising him, even though he has his hands behind his back. This time I can give a positive identification. When I leave to make my statement he looks even more nervous than before.

Once Dad and David have done their part our ordeal is over for the day. We can go on holiday tomorrow as planned. The police have made another appointment for the parade that was cancelled: 6 May, after our return from the south of France. It is not the most relaxing thought to take away on holiday. I have never flown before and am nervous enough already. Still, total strangers have been kind enough to offer us their holiday apartment, and various people, including the Ealing Eagles, the American football team, have sent us gifts of money. We all need a break. The money will pay for the flight. All I need to do is sit back and enjoy myself. The flight is not as bad as I expect. I'm not too keen about the pain in my ears on takeoff, otherwise it is OK. I am worried about David's perforated eardrum, but he assures me there is no problem. Why am I so uptight?

We arrive in France during a mistral, the cold northwesterly wind that can bring temperatures well below freezing point even though the skies are clear. Apparently it can last for varying lengths of time but this one is only just beginning. Great. It will be just like North Wales in summer, though I've never sat on the beach doing my knitting in a coat before. Princess Anne is coming to open the new YMCA buildings when we get back home and we have been invited. I am determined to finish in time for the occasion the pink jumper I took to the identification parades.

The apartment is only a few minutes' walk from the sea, and on the two good days it is very pleasant on the beach. David goes swimming. He still isn't back to full strength, his arms and legs took such a bashing, and I'm sure he isn't meant to get his ears wet, but there is no telling him.

One day we walk to the far side of the bay and take a boat trip to St Tropez. This time the sun is shining, but I have come prepared for the worst and have far too many clothes on. We walk around the harbour, inspecting how the other half lives. There is little else to do. The season hasn't really started yet, lots of places are still closed. Not that it would make much difference if they were open: everything is very expensive and both of us are still on the dole. Dad is in his element, though. He loves French cuisine, and is quite happy to go off and do his own thing.

I wish David would occasionally, too. I am finding the holiday a considerable strain. I speak French, but not well enough to be comfortable using it. David doesn't speak the language at all, and the locals have great difficulty understanding his English, so we are thrown into one another's company too often. I have said 'yes' to his proposal, but it is not official. Nobody knows. Not even my dad. I still wish at times that I could get away by myself. Or have some female company. I need other people to talk to who were not so directly involved. Women friends. I never expected to hear myself admitting that. Men are not exactly flavour of the month at the moment. I still find Dad difficult and being just the three of us together again puts me straight back into the situation I would rather forget. The identity parades haven't helped. Everything has come flooding back.

I'm worrying now whether I've got the right man or not. Was the man I identified really Man 3, or could it have been Man 2? I keep waking up in the night with it all going round in my head. Man 3 or Man 2? Man 2 or Man 3? If I haven't got the right person it could mess up the whole thing. I need to see the other man to be sure. He is still a shadow, a bulky outline in a grey patterned jumper from the scenes on television when they were taken to court. I have these images of bodies huddled under blankets. Bystanders banging on the roof of the van shouting abuse. A muddle of surnames. Ages. Nothing else. I need to know. To see a face. Put a name to that face. Dispel the ghost. I know least about the one who is most important in my case. He is too much of a mystery. I want to know what he looks like in normal circumstances; to get rid of the misty pictures in my mind and replace them with something real. I know he is a few months older than me, though I was delighted to discover he was not born in the same year. That isn't a lot to go on. I need more information to put it together in my mind. Yet the thought that I might see him in a couple of weeks fills me with dread.

It was good of people to offer their homes, but this is not the right place for me at the moment. There is too much time to sit and think. I would be better doing things. I am not used to so much inactivity. David is quite happy to laze on the beach. I spend my holidays organising beach games and barbecues for hordes of energetic children in my beloved Wales. If I want to be anywhere it is there, but the house we use was not offered. It is another sadness. I will live with it. I am ungrateful and out of sorts; 6 May probably has much to do with it. Once that is over, maybe life will return to normal for a while.

CHAPTER FOURTEEN

By the time the dreaded date arrives I am a bag of nerves. I have convinced myself I was correct about Man 3. The person still to be identified has to be Man 2. Dad rings the police to check that all is in order. It isn't. There has been another problem and the identification has been cancelled. The only option now is a confrontation in court. I will not see Man 2 until then. I am not surprised at the cancellation. I feel as if nothing will have power to shock or amaze me any more – though I would be fascinated to know why we have been invited to the official opening of the YMCA after the way I left it.

I finish the jumper on time and wear it to the ceremony. Dad conducts the prayers and has a long chat with Princess Anne afterwards. She is obviously aware of the attack, and expresses her family's concern for our family. I stay in the background. After all, nobody knows who I am. Do they? I am sometimes not sure myself. Back in March there was no time to think or feel. Now there is too much. Being unemployed is giving my body the space it needs to recover. My mind is a different matter. It keeps getting stuck on the same subject. I would be better working. I apply for an administrative post at a church in London. The people interviewing me know my father and make some comment about him and David. I refer to myself as 'the victim'.

'One of the victims,' they correct.

It is not what they say but the way that they say it. Their tone implies that what I have been through is not as significant as everyone has made out. I cannot handle it. I feel bad enough about myself already. I don't need anyone to take away the tiny shreds of confidence I still have. The police have worked so hard to bolster my self-esteem, to tell me I am special, important to their case. It has all been stripped from me. I am back where I started.

On the Tube going home I feel that everybody is looking at me again. They know I was the victim. It was in the papers. They saw my photo. The carriage is full, but I feel very conscious of being on my own. An outcast. Why should anyone want to know, or employ, me? All they can do is stare. The train has to pass Wormwood Scrubs. The accused men are being held there. It is my fault. I am useless, worthless. At White City I have to change trains. I stand on the edge of the platform as the train thunders towards me. I only need to take one step and I would no longer have to worry what anyone thinks.

I cannot do it. Some poor driver would have to live with the trauma for ever, and it would cause chaos for the commuters. Pug's little episode on the Underground delayed everybody for half an hour or more. I dread to think how long it would take to remove the mess I would make. It is frightening enough to think I could even consider it.

I need Peter to give me a hug, and tell me I am not as bad as those people have made out. He would know what to say to make me feel good about myself again. He would also be extremely upset about all that has happened. It is better he does not know. He has been spared that burden. So has my grandma.

When I get home I lock myself in the bathroom and cry everything out of my system. It is becoming a fairly regular habit. If I don't get a job soon to break the pattern of despair I look like having a very soggy summer. Sainsbury's come to the rescue. Pug has already done her preliminary training at the store where Princess Diana does her shopping. Now she is working in a new branch in Chiswick. I join her in June. The manager used to be in charge at the store where Mum works so he understands the situation and is very friendly and helpful. They put me on the bakery for the first few days, sealing buns in plastic bags. It is not exactly mind-stretching. If anything, I have even more time to think. Fortunately, someone in the cash office decides to leave and I manage to get a transfer. Counting money is a definite improvement; I have to concentrate on that.

Dad and David go to the preliminary court hearing. I am not required. The police inform me that they try not to use rape victims until it is absolutely necessary – to spare them yet another ordeal. I'm glad someone is considerate, but there's no need for them to worry about my feelings. I am only one of the victims. Nobody significant. Besides, I would rather like to go to court. I still know so little about Man 2. Seeing him might set my mind at rest. I am not allowed. End of story. If only it was. When Dad and David get home after the hearing I have only one question: 'What were their names?' I really mean, 'What was his name?' They don't know.

I lapse back into apathy. The weeks pass. Life happens, but it has no meaning. Just greyness, nothingness. I go through the motions but it's all mechanical. As a group of us are going out to the fair one day, a passerby brings me back to earth with a jolt:

'That's the house where it happened.'

It is better being a zombie. Safer. A zombie doesn't have any feelings. It can't be hurt. It doesn't worry whether it's a victim, it doesn't feel guilty every time a rerun of 6 March flashes across its memory. There are so many whys and if onlys. Why didn't I do anything to stop it happening? If only I had been wearing something different. Did I lead them on? Encourage them in some way? What else could I have done to prevent it, other than not be there?

A further anxiety gnaws at the back of my brain. Will I ever be able to enjoy sex when all I have known is the horrific? The need to experience the good is very strong. The offer is there if I want to take it up, but it goes too much against the grain. Besides, my body has suffered enough indignities. The prodding and poking of the various medical examinations have done nothing for my self-image. There are times when I feel like a sack of potatoes, being humped around at someone else's whim. It's enough to put anyone off for life.

I go to Wales to work on the holiday mission. The leader puts me in charge of a group to 'take my mind off things'. A major crisis does exactly that for a few hours, then the self-accusation starts again. In such a beautiful place I feel even more ugly. Scrubby has been cleaned. The blood has gone from his ear and he is nearly as good as new. I wish the same could be said of me. All the washing in the world will not restore me to my former condition. I am nothing but a blot on the landscape.

I stand on the clifftop, looking across the bay to the mountains and the long, low line of Anglesey. My white skirt billows in a breeze coming up from the sea. I bought it in the spring to go with the pink jumper for Princess Anne's visit. At the time I didn't think of the significance of the colour. Now I feel I am deceiving myself by wearing it. I am not pure, unsullied. I am second-hand. Like the clothes we so often had to wear as children. Nobody knew where they came from, but I always felt there was a slight stigma attached to them.

The depression I have been fighting off all summer is not lifting as people hoped. In fact, it is intensifying. My relationship with David is not going well. Working with a group of like-minded people is showing up just how far apart we have been drifting in our thinking. When we first started going out he was an agnostic, but he was prepared to discuss things. He even came to church with me. After the rape he changed. He couldn't accept that a God of love could let something like the attack happen to one of His children. He wanted to see a miracle. I told him his recovery had been one. I never expected to see him out of hospital within eight days after being on the critical list. He puts his recovery down to medical science and rejects the influence of people all over the world praying for him.

To make matters worse he has been turned down by the police force on medical grounds. He is very angry. The hospital had told him he was OK. A territorial army medical passed him as fit. The police don't agree. He worries that he hasn't been told the whole truth. He could be right; his hearing is definitely becoming weaker in the damaged ear. He is restless and unsettled. I know the feeling well. We are no longer able to talk about spiritual things. Neither can we talk about the subject that is always uppermost in my mind. Not in the depth I now need. David feels useless, inadequate. There are few books on the subject, neither of us have really had much to do with the advice agencies, and people are beginning to switch off when the subject crops up. We are on our own. David at least understands what I have been through. If our relationship breaks up there will be no one. No other man will be interested in me. I am scared. The one person who loves me enough to want to marry me is no longer on the same wavelength. What is there left to live for?

Immediately after the attack life seemed so precious, so important. What has happened? Why do I feel so dreadful now, in this place which has always been so healing? Why didn't you let me die, God? If I was dead I wouldn't have to cope with the memories. Death must be easier. It would all be over in an instant. I am in the right place. There are no rush-hour crowds. Only the waves pounding on the rocks below. People will be upset, but they will recover. I'm not much of a loss.

It would distress the children, though, maybe scar some of them for life. I turn from the temptation a second time, but I am exhausted. Totally and utterly. It is back to trusting. There is nothing left of me. You will have to take over, God, and put me back together. I can't carry on alone. I haven't even got the energy to walk over the edge of the cliff.

Other people on the team stay blissfully unaware of how I feel. Apart from Shirley, who is sleeping in the bunk underneath me. I have not had a nightmare since I was about ten years old. Now I have two. The first night it is a kind of *Back to the Future* experience. Someone I know is about to go out on a motorbike wearing a silver helmet. I have seen it all before. I know he is going to have a fatal crash, yet I cannot stop him. It would be wrong.

Apparently I have been tossing and turning, hurling myself about the bed. Shirley has had nearly as rough a night as I have. The fact that others already know about my disturbed night means I am able to share my anxieties. It is not just the images, but the arguing with myself in a semiconscious state that has left me exhausted.

The second night I dream I am watching myself dying. It is no more peaceful than the first nightmare. Shirley will be wishing me back in Ealing if I carry on in this fashion. In all other respects I seem all right. Physically I look the same. What else could be wrong with me — apart from my lack of modesty when changing? That has provoked more than a few comments. It is something I am obviously going to have to relearn. The various medical examinations have taken any shreds of modesty that remained after the attack. In the end I gave up and thought, 'Let them all look. Why should I care? I had no say in the initial action.' Sharing a room with several females who have obviously never seen anything more shocking than the school communal showers is teaching me a little more restraint, although whether they would agree about that is a different matter. I always seem to switch on the waterworks in Wales, and even in the busyness of the mission I am able to cry some of the stockpiled hurt out of my system. By the end of the fortnight God is much more in control.

On the last evening there is a spectacular sunset. When activities are over the leader and I walk up the mountain to return some keys to the caretaker, then sit chatting for a while.

RAPE – My Story

He wants to know what I intend to do about my relationship with David. It's a good question. A lot of people have advised me not to stay with him just because of what's happened. Others seem to think it would be nice if everything went well and we could get married. I am in total confusion. I don't want to hurt David, and I don't want to throw away what may be my only offer of marriage, but is that sufficient basis for a lifelong commitment? I think not. I love him as a person but I don't feel I am in love with him. Not sufficiently to pursue the relationship. The leader may not know it, but I have been begging for someone to give me some clear guidance, to ask the right kind of questions. They all seem to have given up after the initial rebuffs they received from me. The leader is quite right. I can no longer sit on the fence.

David has been staying in the Vicarage while I've been away. He knows I am due back, but when I get home he has gone out drinking with his pals. He doesn't improve the situation on his return. He mistakes me for Pug. Thanks, Dave, that's just the kind of confidence booster I need.

Breaking with him is still incredibly hard. He had mapped out our life in his own mind. He was going to join the police force. Then we would be married. Like all the best stories, we would live happily ever after. Instead he has been rejected by the police, and I am trying to tell him that I want to end our relationship. He finds it hard to take and does not agree that we are drifting apart. Couldn't we stay together until after the court case?

I have received the summons to appear as a witness for the prosecution when the case comes before the Old Bailey, but no date has been set as yet. In London it can take around twelve months. Only six have passed so far, though it seems like a lifetime. I could not spend another six months in no-man's-land. It is better to make a clean break, but I hope we can stay friends. David has been such an important part of my life. I dread to think what it will be like without him.

CHAPTER FIFTEEN

David and I have split. The relationship staggered on for a few days after my return from Wales but it obviously wasn't working. It had to come to an end. David's words on parting have made me feel awful, though:

'If ever you need me, I'll be waiting.'

Now I feel guilty on three scores: agreeing to marry him, breaking up, and letting him get involved with me in the first place. If we had never gone out together he wouldn't have been in the Vicarage, he wouldn't have got hurt, and he wouldn't have had all his plans messed up. Friends try to persuade me that he made choices as well, but I'm not convinced. I feel I have used him. I needed stability so much after what happened, it was almost inevitable I would say 'yes' when he proposed. I was so vulnerable; I had to have some kind of hope. The knowledge that somebody loved me was like an anchor, a lifeline. I can see, though, that it was probably unfair of him to ask me at that point. There was so much whizzing round in my head: pregnancy, abortion, adoption. Nothing else really mattered. I should never have accepted his offer, but I was incapable of thinking clearly.

I still am, for that matter. There are days when I ask myself, 'What have I done? Have I thrown away my only chance of marriage?' Now I am on my own. No one else has come rushing into the gap. I miss David. I could talk to him, he knew what

I'd been through, even if we couldn't go into details, or talk about the things that are eating me away from inside.

At least the papers never got hold of the specifics of the rape. I don't think I could ever lift up my head again if people knew the kind of things that happened. Let's hope the majority of the population are as innocent as I was about all that rape can involve. As it is, the Press Council have given the papers a rap over the knuckles about some of the things they printed, but I doubt it will have any effect. All they can say is 'naughty little people'. The damage has already been done.

Harry Greenway is still pursuing the matter through Parliament. He is trying to ensure anonymity for rape victims from the time a crime is reported. It's good to know someone cares enough to try to do something, and it will be worth it if other women in a similar situation are protected better than I was. People knew my family's name, where we lived, how old I was (depending on which paper they read), even my choice in clothes and hairstyle, almost from day one. Yet I still don't know any more about the man who attacked me. There has to be something wrong.

I am not going to think about it. Or about David. I am going to look forward, not back. There's only one small problem. The trial hangs on the horizon like an ugly black cloud. Perhaps looking forward isn't such a good idea. I will concentrate on the here and now.

It works for all of four weeks – till Pug comes to meet me on my way home from work one Thursday in early October. The house has been burgled again. I almost laugh with disbelief. It is exactly seven months since the last time. What's so special about our house?

Inside the Vicarage I am greeted by the familiar sight of tipped-out drawers, police officers, and silver fingerprint powder. One of the police officers who worked on the original case is there. It is good to see him, but sad to hear he is leaving the force. This time the police have not been able to find many prints and think teenagers must be involved. Not a great deal has been stolen. The caretaker of the local school raised the alarm when he heard glass being smashed. I shouldn't have been so scathing in my reaction to the Neighbourhood Watch scheme after all.

I walk round the house surveying the damage. It all seems so futile. My pottery piggy bank lies in pieces on the floor, but none of the money has been taken. A Chocolate Buttons money box has been stamped on. I pace restlessly around, still hunched in my coat and making sarcastic remarks. A useful cover-up. No one must know how badly I am hurting inside. It has taken me straight back to 6 March, only more so. This time there isn't the numbness to take the edge off my feelings. No way am I parting with my coat. Ever since childhood coats have been a symbol of security. If ever I needed security it is now.

I am supposed to be going to a meeting, but I cannot cope with facing people. Telephones are safer; no one can see my face. I dial one of the numbers I have used so often that I know it by heart. There is no one there, nor at the next number, nor the next. Eventually I do manage to find someone home. We talk for a while but it isn't enough. I need someone I trust here with me. Someone to talk through the fears, and exorcise the ghosts, especially in my room. Another stranger has been in. Uninvited. I don't even know what he looks like. To make matters worse, I have only just changed the room around to help get rid of some of the memories from the first time. What else can I do? People are amazed that I am able to sleep in it at all. No one has stopped me so far. It is my room. No one is going to stop me now. But it is a hard battle.

I take a bath and howl out some of my anger and frustration, then lie on my bed in the darkness. I need a hug, but there is no one to comfort me. I am on my own. There is no Jim this time. No David. Only you and me, God. And I'm not doing too well. You're going to have to help me. Please.

When we take stock there are only a few things missing.

There's not a lot to steal in the first place. Mum's bits and pieces of jewellery that the police managed to recover have gone again. So have my chain and a gold bracelet Joe gave me. We can live without those. It's not what's been stolen that's upsetting me. The loss of my fragile security is far more damaging. People have been inside the Vicarage again. In my room. They know where everything is. What is there to stop them coming back?

I do not have a very restful night. In the morning I am tired and edgy, but I have no intention of staying in the house all day. I am better at work. We must carry on as normal – if that is ever going to be possible. The people I work with are sympathetic when I explain we have been burgled again, or at least some of them are. One of my colleagues tells me I 'invite trouble'. I can hardly believe my ears. I was at work when it happened, yet she is telling me it is my fault. Perhaps she's right. Is there some fatal flaw in my make-up? She certainly seems to think so. Maybe others think that as well, but are too polite to say so.

The morning drags. I need that hug more than ever. My body is in Sainsbury's; my mind is back in March, reliving the fears and anxieties. I try to lose myself in my work, but I cannot stop yawning. The others think I am tired or have a headache because I am so quiet. They can think what they will. I would be out of here like a shot – if I had the energy to lift myself out of my seat. I am glad when lunchtime comes. A couple of the staff are celebrating a birthday. That should take my mind off things. It doesn't. Before long I find myself talking about the two burglaries. If I'm not careful people are going to grow bored by the same tune. It seems OK this time, but the girls I am with are shocked. They didn't even know about the first occasion. I wondered about that from the way they have been talking about a rape on one of the television soap operas. Rape seems to be the 'in' topic in magazines and on television. Both *Brookside* and *EastEnders* have been running story lines on the subject. Let's hope they manage to increase people's awareness of the trauma involved. It might be a good idea if it was compulsory viewing for some people.

The afternoon passes with slightly less hassle and when I return home the house is nearly back to normal. The fingerprint lady has stacked the change from my piggy bank in small piles, and I can now close some of the drawers that have been pulled open. The smashed pig still lies on the floor. I am not going to clear it up. It has yet to sink in properly. I need to assimilate it before I can move on.

When Saturday comes I just want to sleep, but it isn't possible. I am expected at work. In some ways I'm glad to go. I'm still not sure if I will ever be able to feel safe in the house again. The local paper has printed a report of the burglary, commenting that our house is secluded and we have few neighbours. It isn't the first to be so explicit. I wonder why they don't just give the keys away. It would save the cost of replacing the glass.

Work isn't an improvement. I should have stayed in bed. I am placed with different people and I don't think I have ever spent a day where the general conversation has been so coarse and disgusting. Yet these are people at managerial level. I liked one quite a lot. Until now. I wasn't aware he found jokes about bestiality and buggery so amusing. I certainly don't. I want to be sick, to walk out, to shout, 'Buggery is not amusing. It's hell.'

I force myself to stay, but only just. Am I being hypersensitive? Is there something wrong with me? Who are they trying to impress? These are my bosses. People I have respected. Is it naïve to expect a basic level of decency? Should I tell them how hurtful their language and conversation is?

I do try to talk with one later but he doesn't seem to understand. The jokes and innuendoes continue. The only way I can handle it is by being brusque, or ignoring him. It is not a good way of resolving the problem, but the wounds have gone deep. In some ways this burglary has been worse than the other.

When everybody expected me to fall to pieces I didn't. Now that I have, people have lost interest. I have to wait until Sunday before a doctor in the congregation at church gives me the hug I have been longing to receive.

CHAPTER SIXTEEN

Jim is coming to stay. It will only be for one night, but I am so looking forward to his visit. It seems weeks since I saw him. I have straightened out a little bit since the burglary but flashbacks are far too commonplace for my liking. Perhaps he will help me get things back in proportion. The trouble is there are so many things that can trigger an attack: rubber gloves, Radox, kitchen knives, the silver fingerprint powder that refuses to come off some of the furniture. One minute I am plodding on with life quite happily, the next I am living 6 March all over again.

I am invited to a party by the officer who is leaving the police force. I want to go, even if it's only to buy him a drink and thank him for all that he has done. It's good to see the police relaxing off duty. I have not had such a good time for some months. Quite a lot of the people at the party were working behind the scenes in March. One of them knocks the ground from under me whilst we are chatting. He has actually met me before. On the doorstep, the day of the attack. For some reason that image has been very vivid in the past few days. The police coming to the door, me staggering towards the ambulance, people watching, commenting. It was awful. I was not a pretty sight. I ask him to erase it from his memory. To remember me how I am, rather than the state he saw me in then.

There's hardly anyone at work now who is not aware how

delicate certain subjects are as far as I am concerned. It doesn't make a lot of difference. Buggery still seems to be at the forefront of people's conversations. Even a discussion on morality ends up with people using the same sick comments and phrases. I sit there and think, if only you knew. But they do. I try to change things, but it's uphill work. Is it so unrealistic to expect people to have some sensitivity?

I am surviving, but only just. I am learning techniques to help me cope with the worst times. When the house creaks and I think it's people walking about I turn on the radio. Night-time radio is never particularly stimulating, but it does give me a bit of comfort and reassurance and helps to stop me feeling so afraid. Other times I switch myself to overdrive – the mechanical side that remembers little and blanks out a lot. I go to a Christian event with my parents. One of the comperes passes on people's prayers and concern for the family. I think flippantly, Did something happen? I wonder what it could be?

It is all a defence mechanism, a way of insulating myself from further hurt. As far as that is possible. There are so many gaps in my defences. Jim is not coming. His car has been stolen; the police have found it burnt out. His guitar, tapes, books, keys, have just gone up in smoke. All that remains is a rainbow patch that was on the robes he used when he was leading church services.

I could go and chat with the doctor, but she must be getting sick of the sight of me. I have been backwards and forwards so many times over the past few months. When I was little doctors always seemed to know their patients. As I got older and practices got bigger no one ever seemed to know my identity. They know me now all right. They must think I'm a real hypochondriac, with all the different symptoms I keep presenting to them.

The pains in my ribs and chest persisted for at least four months after the attack. I had a second X-ray, but there was still no sign of anything wrong so my GP sent me to a specialist.

The pain had gone by the time my appointment came round but I still went to see him. It had done that once before, then come back again. The specialist kept me waiting for hours, then all he could suggest was that I should play squash and see a psychiatrist.

I left the room not feeling very polite in my mind about that man. I had guessed it would be only a matter of time before someone suggested my problems were psychosomatic. He can forget the psychiatrist. I don't like people who delve into minds. The pains in my chest and ribs were there before the attack. I prefer my own GP's interpretation that I must have strained a muscle and the tenseness in my body means that it hasn't been able to heal properly. Only recently has she told me how concerned she was about my health earlier in the year. She had thought I might be developing pleurisy or pneumonia.

Part of the problem is that there's so little contact between the different agencies involved. I am constantly finding myself repeating information I have already given to the GP at the clinic or the hospital, and vice versa. Everything takes so long to go through the official channels. It doesn't exactly ease my state of mind when I have to keep spelling out all the gory details in triplicate. I want to forget, not be continually reminded.

If only it were possible. There's my period for starters. I've always hated it; now it's a positive nightmare. Every four weeks I go through the same old ritual: Am I pregnant or not? I shall be glad when December gets here and the nine months are over. Then I shall know definitely. At the moment I swing from one extreme to the other. On the one hand, I have the monthly evidence to prove I can't possibly be. On the other, I cling to the hope I could still bear a child. I tell myself people are sometimes pregnant despite all the signs to the contrary. Then I start imagining that I will go into labour and it will result in a total collapse of my uterus. Am I just broody? Or is it a subconscious inability to believe I will ever be pregnant? Or that I deserve to be? Perhaps the specialist is right, I should see a psychiatrist. Surely it can't be natural to be thinking these things?

As if that isn't enough, I've also got trouble with anal tearing and bleeding. It doesn't hurt much physically, but emotionally it is hell. Straight away I think buggery, buggery, buggery. The GP has mentioned the possibility of having the vein causing the problems cauterised. I wish somebody would do something. I don't want to have to live with this for the rest of my life. It always seems to come at the most inconvenient times. Bank holidays are a speciality. Just as the doctor's surgery closes.

Blood in my mouth is even worse. I've had a gum disease recently. Every day I wake up with a mouthful of blood. It makes me want to retch. I talked to a hygienist at the dental surgery but she said it would go away, it was no great problem. It might not be to her, it is to me. I hate anything to do with blood. The sight of it is bad enough. The taste of it is even more revolting. If I cut myself I can't lick my finger to stop it bleeding. I used to be able to do it. Not any more. I have to get to some water, and wash it away.

When I hit the worst patches I sleep a lot. Ever since I was sixteen I've slept out my hassles. They don't seem so important once I've had a nap. I don't know what started it off, whether it was exam trauma, or what. People sometimes think I'm lazy because I need so much sleep. They don't know what it's like to feel totally and utterly exhausted, to have no energy for anything. Because I look OK they think I'm fine. They can't see that I might be putting up a good front but that I'm cracking up inside. They'll say things like, 'I'm exhausted too'. It's not the same as emotional exhaustion.

My GP recommended that I have a year off work, but it gets so boring stuck at home. It's a blessing she's so understanding, I don't know where I would be without her. She goes out of her way to be helpful. I certainly don't want to end up on tranquillisers, feeling out of this world entirely. One of my friends was taking eight a day at one point. I saw the effect they had on him. I was offered Valium when I had my wisdom teeth out but I wouldn't touch it even then. Thankfully nobody has pressurised me, or sat there writing prescriptions before I can explain what's bothering me. I must go and see the doctor again. This time I have a cold sore. Nasty, yucky thing. She will know what to do about it.

Unfortunately my own GP is not available. The doctor I see is not worried about little things like cold sores. Or medical notes. He thinks I am Pug, and talks to me accordingly. I bite my tongue and get out of the surgery at the first possible opportunity. I head for the park in tears. It's the one where I was followed but today that is a minor consideration. I pace the paths for hours before eventually collapsing on a bench and howling my eyes out. I am concerned about the cold sore, but I am also desperate to talk. How many clues do I have to keep giving people?

I decide to go and see my friends at the police station. They usually know what to do on these occasions. When I have composed myself sufficiently I drag myself the couple of hundred yards to the main road and up the concrete steps to the front door. There is no one I recognise on duty at the main desk. I ask to see any of the three or four people who have been such a strength to me in the past. None of them are there. The desk sergeant enquires if I would like to talk to anybody else. He wants to know if I am all right and seems reluctant to let me go. I must look in an even worse state than I thought.

Eventually I manage to persuade him that I am OK. It works with him, but I'm not going home till I have calmed down a bit and made myself more respectable. I wander around the shops in Ealing Broadway, trying to gather my thoughts together. Should I see a psychiatrist? I'm not keen on the idea, but I've got to talk these things through with someone. What if they start probing too deeply? We did a bit of psychology when I was training for nursery nursing at college. I find Freud's theories frightening. I don't think it really follows God's pattern.

Surely, trusting God means just that? Not pulling things to pieces and working out how it all happened. If I had a broken leg it would be much simpler. Physical damage is so much easier to handle.

What shall I do, God? People seem to think it will do me good. No one else can offer much help. They're all busy with other things. It's back to you and me. What are we going to do about it? I know it's no use asking 'why?' It has happened. You can't turn the clock back; there's no point regretting what can't be changed. Just get me through. But does that really mean having to see a psychiatrist?

CHAPTER SEVENTEEN

I step out of the lift on the third floor of the hospital. I can see signs pointing to the Psychiatric Department. Is anyone watching to see which way I go? I am carrying a massive bag containing my uniform for work and I don't want anyone to think I am being admitted. It's bad enough having to come here in the first place. I sit nervously in reception, waiting my turn. Everyone else seems very weird. It's hard to tell which are the patients and which are the doctors. I shall be glad when I am safely back in Sainsbury's. I've never been able to handle mental illness. In my worst dreams I never imagined I might need treatment one day.

Once I am actually talking to someone it's not nearly as bad as I expected. The doctors are female and they simply ask a few questions, without making any assumptions. A kind of assessment session I suppose, nothing too intimidating, despite the surroundings. The room I am interviewed in is stark and bare, apart from some lighting equipment and a television camera which are most off-putting. The doctors keep telling me not to worry, the camera isn't in use. That's as maybe, but it doesn't exactly help me to relax. We even had to fight over who should get the decent chair. By the end of the session I feel slightly encouraged, but quite wobbly. I have been advised not to attempt to go to work, but being me I know best, or think I do. I regret it later.

Pug comes with me on the second visit. The doctors seem to think we could both be helped so we have several joint sessions. I am very glad that she is there on one occasion. While we are waiting for our appointment a strange-looking man comes in shouting for a specific doctor. He has three sets of martial arts weapons and is hurling the largest in the air. The staff haven't a clue what to do. There are only two women behind the desk, and no men anywhere in sight. The women call security and do their best to pacify the man, but I think they are as frightened as we are. It's a great relief when our two doctors come down the corridor and usher Pug and I out of the way. By the speed they are moving they obviously have no intention of arguing with the man. Not that I blame them. All the talk of equality is fine in theory, but an unarmed woman has no chance against an unstable man, especially if he has some form of weapon. We are very glad when we catch a glimpse of the security guards coming to the rescue at last, several minutes after they were summoned.

The incident makes me even more glad that I don't have to attend too often, although it is an enormous relief to be able to talk through my feelings about wanting to be pregnant. The doctors seem to think it is quite normal and reasonable. They even suggest pregnancy could have been the one good thing that happened as a result of the rape. I'm not at all convinced. I can see that a baby would divert my energy, but I'm still appalled I could even consider such a possibility in these circumstances.

I would like to talk further about knowing how to relate sexually if the situation ever arises in the future, but they don't seem to think it will be a problem. I wish I had their confidence. It used to worry me even before I was raped, now heaven only knows how I will handle it. Buggery is an even bigger obstacle. I doubt I will ever be able to tell anyone how I really feel about that. I certainly can't cope with going into the details at the moment. I am depressed enough already. I don't want these people poking around my life any more than is absolutely necessary.

Talking about the loss of my hymen comes more naturally. The doctors seem to think that event is just as important as I do. I'm not some freak from a past century after all. If women can experience sadness as a result of losing their hymen by choice, I am perfectly entitled to be depressed. I am not abnormal, just an ordinary human being coping with the loss of something that is important to her. I have to mourn that loss. I need to cry about it, get angry, go through all the feelings normally associated with mourning. It makes sense. I know a bit about bereavement and the fact that people go through various stages, although no one can specify exactly how, or when. Apparently I have been doing some of the things instinctively, which is reassuring. Perhaps there is hope for me after all?

When we get on to the subject of the men I am not quite so certain. Various people have suggested that the rapist should be castrated, but that's not on my agenda. It smacks too much of 'an eye for an eye, a tooth for a tooth', but I did reconsider my ideas on capital punishment for a while. I would certainly be happier if I knew he wasn't going to attack anyone else, but what happens if the courts convict the wrong person? I'm not one hundred per cent convinced it's a real solution, although it might be more of a deterrent.

Sentencing can be so lenient at times; I only hope the courts give the people involved in our case a proper sentence. Not out of vengeance, but so that justice can be seen to be done. Nobody wants a rapist on the streets, that was obvious from the publicity. So many people have spoken out against what happened, have demanded severe punishment for the men for what they did. Dad was making his views known even before he was out of hospital. We actually seem to be in agreement on this subject. Justice and forgiveness are not incompatible.

My image of men has taken a beating, though. I've always thought of them as some kind of supermen. Strong. Able to do anything. Faced with weapons, the two who could have protected me had no more resources than I did. Somehow I have to sort out which bits of my image are true, and which I would do better to leave out. I've never really thought about how Dad and David felt about letting me down. I've been too busy coming to terms with what has been going on inside me.

The doctors have suggested that all the important men in my life have let me down in some way. Pete is dead, Jim has moved, another friend has gone away to college. They are right so far, but these things happen. People go away. New people come along. I don't feel let down. Just alone.

I've been accused of taking bitterness to the wrong people. I don't see it in that light. When I get angry there is usually a good reason. I don't think I transfer the bitterness from somewhere else. Neither do I agree with the psychiatrist's verdict that I protect my attackers too much. I don't hate them, and I won't. I hate everything they did, but I also believe that they may want forgiving one day. Sin is sin is sin. God doesn't say one sin is worse than any other. When I met two of the men at the identity parades their reactions showed that they knew they had done wrong.

I'm told I take far more interest in them than I ought to, but if I don't take that responsibility who else will bother? It's going to be far fresher in my mind than anyone else's, and I've seen the reactions when I've asked people to pray for them. I agree with the psychiatrists on one point. They say they don't think it's a natural reaction to be protective to such an extent. I would say it is supernatural. It's only God who is giving me the strength to be concerned about them when other people aren't. The brother of one of the accused has been on a life-support machine for several months now. As I go to sleep I can't help praying for a miracle for him. It's harder praying for the others because it brings it all back, but I do sometimes.

I was worried that the doctors would query my Christian faith, but they reckon they would question it more if I had lost my trust in God as a result of all that has happened. I dread to think where I would be if I had. There's no way I could have come this far. I know He is there, even when there is no one else.

I explained to one of the doctors how I think I am conning myself if I wear white, and that I feel ugly in beautiful places. She told me such feelings are quite common. I was taking the attackers' guilt and I should give it right back. I've been doing just that for a week, and it feels great. Let's hope I can keep up the good work.

The doctors seem to think a lot of my problems stem from my difficulties with relationships. They suggest we should learn to communicate more as a family. Mum and Dad are invited to attend a session. Getting together does help. Somehow we seem a lot closer. I even talk a bit to Dad. Mum astounds me by admitting she has cried, but it's usually when she's alone in the bath. It does seem strange. With Rachel, that's three of us who do it rather than tell anyone how we are feeling. I've certainly never seen Mum cry, even when Grandma died, although she looked as if she could have been crying when she came to the hospital after the attack.

Some of the barriers are coming down, but I think the psychiatrists are only speeding up a process that has already begun. Jim has been telling us for ages that we should talk to each other more. I can see the truth in that, and we have been working on it. Pug's wedding early next year is giving us a new topic of conversation which is not quite so fraught. It's going to be a fairy-tale occasion in the crypt chapel of St Paul's. The doctors seem pleased that we have something positive to look forward to and it's certainly time Pug is the centre of attention for a while instead of me.

Even so, I'm not so sure that delving too deeply into past history is doing too much good at this point in time. If anything, it's compounding my sense of aloneness. I feel it's opening up things that don't need opening up. Or maybe they do, but not now. Some things in my past may not have been wonderful but at least I felt secure. Now I just feel depressed, and having to go to the psychiatrist every few days isn't making me feel any better. I make a joke out of it, but underneath I hate it. It's a sort of defeat, and I could well do without that. I'm going to cancel the last appointment. It's such hard work. It seems more stressful than staying away.

A lot of people have asked if I would like Christian counselling. I would not. We did contact one organisation on David's behalf but I was not at all impressed with the set-up. They claimed to be professional, but ignored a specific request about the payment of fees and the letter they wrote was addressed to the wrong person, covered in Tippex, and looked very scruffy. It made me very cynical. I don't think Christian organisations should accept second-best. They should strive for perfection.

Other Christians have suggested something called 'healing of the memories'. They want me to read certain books and go on various courses, or they offer to introduce me to people who can heal. I shy away from it all. It sounds too pressured. Wham, bam, miracle. I know people can be healed in these ways, but I don't think it's right for me. I'm not asking for instant miracles. I'm very down-to-earth and practical, and I have to go at a down-to-earth pace. Anyway, I believe God *is* healing me. It's just going to take a while. I must remind myself of that when I am in the depths of depression and longing for anything to lift me out.

I usually know exactly who will come to my aid, or think I do. It's always the good-looking men. The trouble is God doesn't always see it in quite the same way as I do. We've had words about that on more than one occasion. There was one particular bloke who annoyed me. He kept cropping up when I felt lousy, saying he had some words from God for me. I didn't want to know. I hadn't been at all convinced by the things various people had tried to tell me before, and it was just after I'd been contemplating suicide, so I felt particularly vulnerable. Besides, he was the wrong person. Or so I thought.

When he at last managed to get past my defence systems he reminded me of the story of the widow woman who felt worthless because she had very little to give, but she gave all she had and it was more than enough. It hit the nail right on the head. I was angry with God for not sending the person I wanted, but He hadn't made a mistake. The message was just what I needed to hear.

CHAPTER EIGHTEEN

At least I now know who my real friends are. Not everybody has stuck by me, but a fair number have, in spite of my finding relationships difficult. According to the experts most people only have two or three close friends but I've discovered I've got a lot more than I thought I had. I don't want to lose them. Especially Jim. It's nothing for us to spend half an hour on the phone. If it's less than that it is purely business. Even so, I must watch it. People will start switching off if I overburden them.

They may not always appreciate it, but talking is by far the best way anyone can help. Or rather, letting me talk. If someone wants to hear what's happened, that's fine by me. I am more than happy to offload my problems. When I find a pair of inquisitive ears I know it is safe to go on. Talking might wear me out, but it provides a real sense of relief. Knowing who can take it, and who can't, is more difficult. Rape is still a taboo subject and people often shy away, or feel sick when they realise I have been a victim. I have to be aware of people's sensitivities, even if they're not always particularly bothered about mine. The last thing I want to do is to give them nightmares, or make them go away and cry. I don't want sympathy. I don't want people to feel sorry. I want them to accept me as I am.

It's even better when it's not totally one-sided. Not that I expect suddenly to be landed with the whole world's problems. There are so many of them: depression, abortion, sexual problems, relatives in prison. People obviously see that I am vulnerable so they feel they can tell me about their own points of weakness. It's not easy, but it's very healing. I am not as alone as I sometimes think. Other people have their own private hell. Once you have someone to share the trouble with it somehow becomes more bearable.

Friends have told me about a girl who was raped three months after me. They want me to talk to her. How on earth am I supposed to set about doing that? I can't just go up to a total stranger and say 'Isn't it a nice day? By the way, I hear you're a rape victim. I'm one too.'

I try to befriend her, but rape's not a subject that comes into polite conversation easily. Eventually someone else breaks the ice. He is friendly with both of us and is amazed by the way we seem to have picked up the pieces of our lives and carried on. He is also convinced we can help one another. He gets us together, says, 'You both know you've been raped. Talk about it.' And leaves us to it. Once the barriers have been removed there is no stopping us. She is thrilled to know she is not cracking up and I am reassured to hear that there is more to sex than the horrific. It is such a relief to be talking with someone who identifies immediately with the problem, and has experienced very similar reactions. The experts were right. The feelings are all part of a normal process of learning to live again.

People have also suggested contacting one of the organisations specifically set up to help rape victims, but we were rather put off when Rachel contacted one of them on our behalf. Their response was to suggest the rapist should be castrated. I have considered phoning the Samaritans a couple of times, but it was just a passing thought. I haven't actually got as far as picking up the phone.

The police have been as much help as anyone. I don't think they warned me about possible aftereffects, such as rape trauma, but they mentioned agencies like Rape Crisis, and they offered to be on call if I needed them. I've always felt I can go back and see them and, apart from that one time when I ended up in Walpole Park, someone's always been around to listen. It's good, because I don't have to pretend with them, they know all the sordid details anyway. There are no barriers; I can be rude to them, and they can be rude back. They're even more like a bunch of friends now. The wife of one was once raped and he is particularly caring and supportive.

Male friends have been very important. I so much need to be able to talk with them, and be hugged by certain ones I can really trust. I probably want to reassure myself that they aren't all monsters. It would be a bit of a blow if they were. I like men, I've always liked them. I don't see why I should have to give up on them now. I don't find it easy to see grown men crying, however. Because I don't cry easily I can't always understand it when other people get upset. That one tear David shed meant a great deal to me, though, and I'm not going to argue if it helps them.

People have been worried how I would react to the rapes that have been shown on the TV soap operas, but after the initial shock I've found them quite helpful. The portrayal of the Sheila Grant rape on *Brookside* was very good, particularly the different reactions she experienced afterwards. The fact that the trauma was ongoing is very realistic; it wasn't all over and done with in a couple of episodes. I think Kathy's rape on *EastEnders* lost a bit of credibility with the bribery, and the fact that it was happening to her for the second time. That really shook me. I've actually thought, 'Well, I've been raped now. So nothing like that is going to happen again.' I've had to stop and face up to the thought that perhaps it could. Rape is becoming more and more common. I can't say it won't happen again. I hope it never will, but I had hoped that it would never happen in the first place.

I would read books if I could find any. There are plenty on bereavement, but very little on the aftereffects of rape. It would be a help if there were some explaining the normal progression –

'This is what happens. These are the stages you go through' – even if it happens slightly differently for each person. I did know a bit, but not enough to help me be properly prepared.

Maybe it's just as well. If I'd known beforehand about the terrible sense of aloneness, it could have blown my mind. I've always been a loner to some extent. I've had to survive on my own, but I've never experienced it quite to this extent. It's tough acknowledging that people can only help me so far. The rest is up to me. There is no way around the feelings. I have to learn to accept them, to be vulnerable. Not that life is all bad. There are incredible amounts of joy mixed in with the pain. God's love is always there, even if I find that hard to accept at times, too. I've always been so much better at giving than receiving. When a phrase from a song reminds me that no one is worthless, we are all special in God's sight, it brings me to a complete standstill. I don't feel at all special, in fact quite the opposite. My gums are bleeding again, and I feel sick tasting the blood in my mouth. I still keep hoping I might be pregnant, and hate myself for it. There's a possibility that the case might go to court in December and I have a picture in my mind that I might give birth in court. Then I could hand the baby to the rapist and say 'Here. It's yours. You look after it.'

I've spoken to Dave and he's not faring too well either. In fact, he's been quite unsettled. Rape does affect men, far more than people are prepared to admit or understand. Men are not supposed to be sensitive. Not that they all are by any means. I shall try to keep up my unofficial education programme. I've decided it's time to end my feud with the boss who upset me with his crude comments. We're both on the defensive still and it's a case of who can get in with an insult first. Not a happy state of affairs. I've told him I want to talk to him, but I never seem to catch him alone. We are rushed off our feet getting ready for Christmas.

A few days into December and the nine months' wait is over.

I am not pregnant, and there is no way I possibly can be. It will be hard to accept, but it's also a great relief. I've had a rough night and feel exhausted, emotionally and physically. Sainsbury's will not be happy, but I take a day off work. When I return one of my colleagues gives me a big hug. One of the bosses undoes the good work almost immediately by remarking that he thought I was away because I was pregnant. He means it as a joke, and has no idea how much it hurts. I change the conversation back to work. Fast.

A date has been set for the trial. We now know it will be at the beginning of February. I am not going to think about it. The Christmas rush should keep me occupied. Instead it makes matters worse. We are short-staffed and I am so tired I can hardly stand up. I need a break but won't be very popular if I take one at this particular point in time. It wouldn't be so bad if I could get a decent night's sleep, but I can't. Once I am in bed I feel even more alone. Every morning the pillow is soaked with my tears.

Perhaps Dad would give me a hug and make things right? No. That would make me too vulnerable. Mum would be better. I pull on my dressing gown and go to find her. She is busy in the kitchen but can spare time for a hug. It's probably the first admission of hurt on my part she has seen. Now she knows something is seriously wrong. After we have talked for a while she makes an appointment with the GP for me. That will make twenty-two trips to ten different doctors, seven blood tests, two X-rays and one short admission to hospital. All in one year.

The doctor suggests a year off work. Again. It would be nice, but I couldn't justify it. She ignores my arguments and signs me off with exhaustion. I manage to stagger through another couple of days before admitting defeat. It has all become too much for me, I know I will be letting them down at work so I chicken out of telling the manager that I won't be back. She thinks I look all right, so how could I possibly be ill? She doesn't know how good I am becoming at disguising my feelings.

I travel up to Rachel's on Christmas Eve and struggle to midnight Communion. Christmas happens. I don't know how. My head aches. I am too tense to sleep, but too exhausted to do much else. All I know is that I want to spend time in Wales. I'm not sure that I want to pray the New Year in again in a hurry, but I do need time to cry, to sleep, to hurt, to heal and to relax. The GP thinks I also need to get David out of my system. She could be right.

Looking back over 1986, it has been quite a year. There's been so much heartache, pain and confusion, but I have come through. There have been good times. They might have been a bit thin on the ground, but there have been sufficient for me to give thanks for the year. God has not deserted me.

Jim is another matter. The first Sunday we are in Wales I make a remark that really annoys him and it shows. It isn't what he says in reply that hurts, but the way his face spells 'Reject'. I have to bite the inside of my cheeks to stop the tears coming there and then. If my best mate rejects me, who is left? I hate crying in public but cannot prevent the tears rolling down my cheeks as I travel back to the house in someone's car. When I was a child, if people got cross with me they always welcomed me back. What if Jim doesn't? It would be more than I could bear.

As soon as we get home I head for the cliff path. If there is no one left I might as well throw myself over the edge. Pete, why did you die? I need you now to give me one of your hugs. The temptations are becoming too great. One of these days I shall do something to end it all. 'Do you hear, God? You've got to save me. I am no longer capable of saving myself.'

Somehow I stumble down the path to the cottages at the end of the beach. I love the sea. Its majesty and might. Its gentleness and serenity. Its ability to give life, or take it away. I only have to keep walking and not look back. But that would make me alone for ever. Even in my deepest moments of despair there has always been God. He gave me my life. Do I have the right to take it? Have I got the strength left not to? It takes courage to face up to life, and energy to have courage. Mine has almost been used up. God, if you want me to go on living, you'll have to give me the energy and the strength.

There is a shout from the cliff. Two of the team are calling me. They'll have to go on calling. Whatever it is no longer concerns me. The two lads start to scramble down the cliffs. They shouldn't do that, it's dangerous. The cliff is very unstable, it could collapse at any time. They are new to the area – they might not know. With a supreme effort I turn towards them. I cannot run. I cannot shout a warning, but I am no longer walking towards the sea.

CHAPTER NINETEEN

We are safely into 1987. I need not have dreaded the New Year quite so much. In many ways it has been a turning point. Jim and I have sorted out our misunderstanding. I've solved my sleeping problem by not going to bed until 3.30. Most amazing of all, I have a new boyfriend. He's one of the lads who came scrambling down the cliffs to my rescue. We're keeping fairly quiet about the relationship for a while, but going out with someone is a very positive step. Just what the doctor ordered in fact, although she may not have foreseen quite such a dramatic turnaround as this.

I can hardly believe it myself. In December I was suicidal. Now I am beginning to enjoy life again. I feel I am over one of the biggest hurdles. I cannot be so unattractive and worthless as I sometimes feel. By the end of January I know I want to marry the new man in my life. Pug had better watch out. She's getting married in March; I might not be so far behind. Not that weddings are my overriding preoccupation. The trial has been fixed for 2 February. Even a new relationship pales into insignificance beside the thought of that. The estimates of how long it would take before the case came to court are not far out. It will be almost eleven months since the attack.

Back in the summer, Carol, the WDI, suggested I should visit the Central Criminal Courts where the trial will be heard. With Dad being Prebendary of St Paul's I'd been in the area several times, but never inside the Old Bailey before. It was quite interesting to watch all the jurors and people going in through the revolving glass doors. Everyone had to have their bags searched and go through a scanning system, including me.

One of the officers based at the Old Bailey took me upstairs to find Carol. She was going through a statement with a girl who was also going to appear as a witness. This one had been stabbed about eleven times, but she was absolutely positive the defence lawyers were going to rip her to shreds. They're not supposed to try to discredit women giving evidence, and her lifestyle was not particularly permissive, but she was petrified that they were going to drag her sexual history through the court and portray her as an immoral woman. She was so worried that Carol had to calm her down. I dread to think how many cigarettes she smoked while she was waiting. We listened to her case and when I heard what the man had done, it was amazing to think she could ever have been concerned over what they would say about her.

Afterwards I was shown around the new courts, and saw the effects of the bombing. Then we got to the oldest part. The painted ceiling outside Court Number One, the central court, is very impressive. Inside the court there is wooden panelling everywhere. My guide explained where everybody sits, and what everything is, including why there is a roof over the witness box. At one time convicted prisoners would go straight from court to the prison beneath, then off in a boat on the Thames to the place where they were to be hung. The smell coming up from the prisons was pretty horrendous and the roof was meant to protect the rest of the court from the worst effects. I told the guide how my great-grandfather had given evidence at the trial of Dr Crippen. It seemed strange to think it was in that very same court.

Before I went home I heard part of another case. That was absolutely horrific, but they made the girl who was in the witness box look as if she was some kind of idiot, the way they were asking the questions. Then and there I determined that if I am called to give evidence there is no way they are going to make me look stupid. I will know everything so well that they won't possibly be able to twist it around. I know I don't have to worry about what they can make of my sexual history, but I have seen the kind of things they can do, and how a woman can be made to feel that she is the one on trial. Especially if it's just her word against the man's.

I certainly don't relish the thought of having to stand up in the witness box in front of everybody. I can understand why people get so uptight about it. There are so many questions that can be used to put people in a bad light. Are you sexually experienced? Are you on the pill? Have you had previous lovers? Or an abortion? Or an illegitimate child? The thing that is worrying me most is if they start pulling me apart about my clothing. Friends keep reminding me I was in my own home, but I've heard how the lawyers can make things sound. They've only got to make a suggestion or two. Wasn't it rather strange to be wearing a summer dress in March? Especially a rather skimpy one? As for a bikini top? Well . . .

The other thing I dread is if they start asking why I didn't try to stop the attack, or suggest that I was actually enjoying it. I did knock the knife to the floor but it seemed that the only other way I could possibly survive was to go along with what Man 2 demanded. We've been told it could very easily have ended up as a murder trial, so I don't think my reactions were unreasonable. What the legal experts might make of it is a different matter.

One of the detective constables on the case explains things a bit more clearly, and allays some of my fears. So does a barrister friend of Rachel's. I actually had a few decent nights' sleep while I was staying with Rachel after our break in Wales, but I am back to the familiar pattern now I am home. The doctor wanted to sign me off work for another four days but I felt I could handle it. After a week of broken nights I am not so sure. I wish I knew what the men have said about it all. Whether their versions of events bear any resemblance to mine. We still don't know how they will plead. In some ways I hope it does go to trial, if only to correct a few of the inaccuracies that have been floating around, and to show how they weren't all involved to the same extent.

There are so many things buzzing round in my head as the dreaded day comes closer. How will I react when I see Man 2? What is his name? Will I have to give evidence? What about David? He will be there. Will he speak to me? Some people think that if I'm at work the worries will go away. They don't. Work might deter them for a while, but that's all. I don't think it's a good idea to bury my head too far in the sand and pretend nothing is happening, even if it were possible. The week before we go to court is constant hassle. Details of the trial seem to change daily from Thursday onwards. Sunday night is particularly rough. I feel very tense and the muscles in my neck are stiff. By Monday morning I have the beginnings of a bad headache but refuse to take any aspirin. I want to have all my wits about me. Some of the congregation are going to spend a couple of hours praying. If ever I needed their prayers, it is now.

Soon after 9 am, Dad, Rachel and I are ushered into the Old Bailey by the back entrance. The press know the trial is on, and want a story. The police assure me they will only be able to print the essential facts. All they are getting from us are the statements we have prepared beforehand, which will be embargoed until after sentencing. Each word has been chosen with enormous care, but there is one line in mine that I am not happy about, and it is to be removed.

My anxieties about that fade into the background when I receive a piece of information I have been waiting nearly a year to know. Someone has told me the name of Man 2. I am quite put out. It is not what I expected it to be. Instead it's one I quite like. How annoying. We still don't know how the men will plead, or whether I will have to have a confrontation with Man 2. The thought does nothing to ease my headache, it's getting worse by the minute. I should have taken a tablet, or brought some with me. All I have is a copy of *Grimm's Fairy Tales*, to help pass the time if we have a long wait.

After some delay while the police find an empty room we are ushered into one on the upper level, well out of the way of the press. The trial is to take place in the court where my great-grandfather was witness. It's good to know that the case is considered important enough to make it to the central court of the land, but it does nothing for the state of my nerves. The judge has been changed at quite short notice, too, which is a bit disconcerting. So is the fact that I still don't know whether I will have to appear as a witness. Surely they must know by now? I send Rachel down to the court to see what she can find out. If the men plead guilty I will be off the hook. If they do not it will go to a full trial. I will be up in the witness box where great-granddad stood.

We have been told that my counsel intends to have a brief word. In the meantime, I must reread my statement. I have no intention of being shown up in court, but it is difficult to concentrate. Barristers are constantly coming in and out, looking for rooms for their clients; the police keep us as up-to-date as possible with information; Rachel pops back to tell us that David and his dad are waiting outside the court downstairs. I have added three pages to my original statement and trying to learn twenty-six pages off by heart in such circumstances, along with a splitting headache, is not the easiest of tasks. A lot of the details have already faded from my memory. Being reminded of them again catapults me back inside the Vicarage to relive it all. I am sick of reading and rereading about the trauma of that day. *Grimm's Fairy Tales* are no diversion. I cannot concentrate. All I want to know is what is happening downstairs. How are the men pleading? What do they look like? Will I have to be a witness? What if I'm sick, or my legs refuse to hold me up?

I try to sleep to release the tension but that only makes my headache worse. Normally I can sleep any time, anywhere. I wish I could go and watch another case, or ring up someone. Anything rather than just sitting here. Waiting. With Dad. He is the wrong person. He keeps trying to make conversation but I don't want to know. Come on. Come on. There's no way I can face this much longer. Ever since that day in the zoo I have hated being alone with big, middle-aged men. 6 March finished me completely. Now I am stuck with one again. I have another to face in court. Not that he would be flattered to think I am calling him middle-aged, he's only a few months older than me.

The clock on the wall must be telling the wrong time. Surely it's later than that? I check it against my watch, it hasn't stopped. An hour passes. An hour and a half. I feel like a prisoner. Trapped. Claustrophobic. I cannot even go out to the loo in case the press start hounding me.

At last Rachel comes to the rescue. Man 2 has pleaded guilty to all the charges. There won't have to be a confrontation. I don't have to appear in the witness box or stay locked in this prison any longer. Man 3 asked that the charge of rape be dropped, but pleaded guilty to all the charges when he was told it would not be. Man 1's lawyer is talking to the judge. He too wants the charge of rape dropped. I am not surprised. Why shouldn't he argue his innocence? I would do the same. Eventually the charge is left on file, but he is not to be tried for that offence. Because it is not going to full trial a jury does not have to be sworn in. The mitigating evidence can begin.

CHAPTER TWENTY

Outside the court there is another delay. If only they knew what the waiting is doing to me. My legs have made it down the stairs, but only just. David and his dad appear in the distance. It's the first time I have seen David since we split up. He looks as nervous as I feel. Now there isn't going to be a trial the police say I am free to talk to him. He has had his hair highlighted, and as we chat I notice that his hearing is very bad. So bad he is even beginning to believe it himself.

The police interrupt us. It is time to go into court. I am under no obligation to attend but I am going, if only to dispel a few of the ghosts. I am aware of a blur of dark gowns, silver and white wigs, police, reporters, people in the gallery above the defence lawyers, the judge in his red robes. To my frustration I cannot get a proper view of the person I most need to see in order to replace the photofit picture with a real man. The wardens are in the way and I dare not stare too hard for fear of what the press might make of it. All I know is I would never have recognised him. He is smart, well-shaven, his hair is decently cut. Quite an attractive-looking young man. Not one who looks capable of doing much harm. Why couldn't he form a normal relationship instead of going to the lengths he did?

The defence lawyers present their version of the factors influencing the way the men behaved. Drugs, alcohol, broken homes, deprived upbringings. Does that really excuse what they did? They must be made to understand they cannot take it out on other people. And there's always the danger they could do the same again under the influence of drugs and alcohol, as is being suggested about Man 2.

David is sitting next to me. He keeps asking what is being said. I don't think you are supposed to talk in court, but it is difficult to hear and there is a lot of shuffling from the press. I repeat what I can without losing concentration on the main events. There seem to be several conflicting stories. One is that the men had planned to break into a big house in a nearby road, but the lady refused to open the door to them so they came on to our house. Another suggests they were only expecting to find the vicar at home and burgle the place. A third implies that Man 2 was aware that a 'good-looking bird' lived at the Vicarage. That is a new one to me. He must mean my sister!

During the lunch break I show a photograph of my new boyfriend to one of the police officers, and look up just in time to see David watching. He knows I am going out with someone else, but says he is unable to have a relationship as he can't come to terms with what men can do to women. I keep trying to forget the extremes of behaviour that have caused us all so much heartache, to replace them with positive images. Today it isn't possible.

Back in court we have to wade through a summary of the main events of 6 March. I wish I could crawl under the nearest bench. The fact that few people really knew what took place allowed me my one remaining shred of dignity. The press are scribbling feverishly. Please God, don't let them print it. The thing I wanted most of all was that nobody should know the full details. It's bad enough that a member of our congregation is here in court. I know he's a policeman and will have heard many horror stories. Does he have to hear mine?

Not that I recognise some of it. Things sound so different in the retelling. The fact that at the beginning they kept referring to me by my first name hasn't helped. I'm always known by my second. I thought they were talking about a different person until the police made sure it was corrected. I felt like standing up and shouting, 'Hey, get it right! It's me you're talking about!'

The only comfort I have is the fact that Man 2 has not disagreed with my statement. Perhaps a trial by jury would not have been so bad after all. At least then I might have seen more of a pattern, a coherent story. As it is, I have to make do with shreds of evidence. A fleeting glance of a pair of pink rubber gloves, a photo, the weapons used. The memories are painful, but I want to know, to discover some sort of sense to it.

The defence lawyers have made a lot of the fact that Man 2 has expressed remorse, and that I have been spared the ordeal of witnessing by the plea of guilty. Fine so far. I do not agree that I have not had to relive it all. What do they think has been happening for the past eleven months? Could they cut themselves off from such memories at the drop of a hat? I have already been forced to remember things I had managed to erase by being here and going through my statement. I know from experience how long it is going to take to blank them out from my mind again. I am well aware how traumatic cross-questioning can be, but I'm not convinced I've been spared that much.

The officer in charge of the case has expressed the opinion that I come from a supportive family, am recovering fairly well, and that it is hoped I will be able to lead a normal life. It's true – as far as it goes. They only know half the story. It feels as though more emphasis is being placed on how a hairdresser in Isleworth provided valuable information about a group of three scruffy men who went to her for haircuts, than on the far-reaching effects all this has had on the three people in the Vicarage, and on their friends and family.

People are growing restless. I guess things are nearly over for today. Sentences will be passed tomorrow, or so I have been led to believe. The judge has decided otherwise. He is going to pronounce some of the sentences here and now. The last thing

I want is to see the men being sent down, but there is no escape. If I get up and leave I will make myself too conspicuous, even supposing I could get past the rows of journalists with pencils poised. All I can do is sit trembling and hope I am not actually sick.

The general impression is that Man 2 will get at least fifteen years. Some think life. The judge takes a more lenient view. He is taking into consideration the fact that I have been spared the ordeal of witnessing, as well as the expression of remorse. If he sentences Man 2 according to the severity with which the public view the crime he would spend a disproportionate length of time in prison for a man of twenty-two. I can hardly believe my ears. He is older than me. What about my life? My prospects? According to the judge the trauma I have suffered is 'not so great'.

He sentences Man 2 to five years for burglary and five years for rape, buggery and indecent assault. Man 3 receives five years for burglary and three for rape. I cannot see the looks on the men's faces as they leave court but I would be very surprised if they were not smiling. It has to be some kind of a joke. So why am I not laughing? Or the people around me? The police, press and my family are absolutely stunned. I am livid.

What did he say? No great trauma? A few trinkets and a video are roughly equal to being taken by force, put through the most revolting sexual acts, and left in total humiliation to discover whether two people you love are dead or alive. To say nothing of the medical examinations, press harassment, risk of infection and the emotional nightmare of the past year. Thank God I have a supportive family. I wouldn't like to say where I would be without them. And why were Pug and I seeing a psychiatrist if it was no great trauma?

The police seem to have most appreciation of how I must be feeling, and close round me as the press gather like vultures, scenting another sensation. How do we react to the sentencing? There has to be a good story here. Quick, get it down. I do not trust myself to speak. Dad knows how to handle the media better than I do. He's already had one session with the television crews. Now he is telling the reporters he will hold a press conference and release statements later. He must do as he sees fit. I just want to be out and away, before something explodes inside me. In the car on the way home the police give vent to the kind of bottled-up fury I would like to express, though in less colourful language. I can understand their frustration and why good officers are leaving the force. After all the effort they have put into the case, and the strain overtime has on family life and relationships.

The next day Pug goes to court. She spent all yesterday sitting by the telephone waiting for news, unable to concentrate on anything else. I would have been the same if I hadn't stayed when I had the opportunity. Now I have no intention of going anywhere near the place again. I want to get as far away as possible – down to the sea. We decide on Poole. Then I can have a hug with my goddaughter at the same time. I am not quite so distressed as I was last night, until a discussion about the sentencing comes on Rachel's car radio. I feel like ringing up the radio station and telling them what I think. Unfortunately there aren't too many phones on the M3.

Walking along the seashore is just the kind of calming experience I need. The sun is shining, but it is still quite cold. We keep on the move – apart from a slight pause while Rachel takes a photograph of me expressing what I think of the judge. Ironically, he comes from this area. A piece of useless information we have somehow gleaned from one of the papers or the radio.

I was right to dread what the press might make of the story. Most of them share our sense of outrage, but they have printed the things I was hoping no one need know. It's hard to think the nation is aching to hear all the gory details, or to see my face on the television news. I don't know which is worse. Becoming public property yet again, or having the bit I wanted embargoed slipping through the net. I do not agree with the sentencing. I agree even less when I hear the sentence on Man 1. Fourteen years. Yet he was the one who tried to help me. No wonder he shouted 'What about the rapist?' as he was sentenced.

Man 1 may have been an experienced burglar, and all that would have had to be taken into account. But wouldn't people rather be burgled than raped? I am not trying to condone crime, but I am convinced that crimes against property have fewer lasting effects than crimes against a person. I am not grieving the loss of my purse twelve months later. All the trauma has been to do with my loss of status, self-worth, my mental and physical well-being. Even outside the Old Bailey Pug heard some men discussing the 'so-called virgin', as if that was what the lawyers had had to say. The hurt is ongoing. There is a constant battle with what others think – the people at work, the papers, passersby, folk on the Tube who look at me as if I have no right to contaminate the air they breathe. Shouldn't things like that also be taken into account? Are they not as important as the mitigating factors for the men involved?

Lord Lane had set up guidelines for rape cases following controversy over lenient sentencing. They suggest a minimum of eight years for an attack in someone's own home with two or more men acting together, with further time for aggravating factors such as repeated rape, the use of weapons and further sexual indignities or perversions. All those features were present. Nevertheless, we are expected to consider the men's youth and the fact that they were led astray by Man 1. If people are old enough to vote and fight in wars at eighteen, surely they should be responsible for their own actions by the time they are nearly twenty-one? To add insult to injury, the men have the right to appeal against their sentences, but there is nothing we can do if we consider them too lenient.

CHAPTER TWENTY-ONE

We are not alone in our anger. According to the papers, Neil Kinnock thinks there is a case for stricter sentencing, Harry Greenway has called for rape cases to be heard by women judges, David wants the rapist castrated, and a spokesman for the Police Federation thinks the sentences are 'woefully inadequate'.

I go to visit Carol. She has been put in charge of a specialised team dealing with rape and child abuse. We chat in the canteen for a while, then she takes me with her to a Cash and Carry and buys me a whole box of Maltesers. Forty-eight packets. She knows that I eat lots of chocolate and crisps but never seem to put on weight. I shall be eating these for the next month. At least the papers have got our opinion of the police correct. I cannot speak too highly of them. It makes me wonder if they really deserve the bad press they so often get, especially now that I know how many things have been reported inaccurately in my own case.

In many ways the press coverage since the court case has been even more difficult than when the rape first happened. People try to tell me that the papers have printed the details to highlight the lax sentencing. Or that the reporters never knew the whole story before and are suddenly realising the full horror of it all. I am not convinced. It's just as likely they saw a whole new range of juicy facts and couldn't wait to sink their teeth in.

I have even appeared on the television news – after all the outcry there has already been about anonymity. We've been told they didn't realise it was me. They thought it was just someone walking past the court. With the widely recognised Michael Saward and David following close behind.

I should think the newspaper coverage will run into several scrapbooks. Reports of the rape, photofits, the arrest of the men, the trial, sentencing, people's reactions. 'So brave victim', 'Too soft judge', 'This cannot be justice', 'Vicar's fury', 'Let down by the law'. It is good to know that other people are as concerned as we are, but I do wish they would let the subject drop now. It seems as if it will reverberate for ever.

Shirley comes to the rescue by inviting me to go on a skiing holiday with her. I only have a fortnight to get ready so it is all systems go. I have been given some money from a special fund by the Bishop of London. That helps to buy most of the clothing I need, but there is no time to do proper exercises or anything. Not that I'm complaining. I will be out of London on *the* day. I warn the leaders of the group from the word go. It's only fair. My reactions might not be entirely predictable around that time. Neither are theirs. One is so upset he goes back to his wife and howls his eyes out. Once we have overcome the initial hurdles it means there is always someone who will listen, which is probably the best gift I could have been given.

Austria is beautiful. When we arrive everything is covered in snow, but I am not the world's best person on skis. I try hard to learn at first, but spend most of the time on my behind. Not the cosiest of places to be when pouring rain is melting the snow. After three days I decide I will be happier just taking things easy. I am content to go walking in the mountains, enjoy the beautiful surroundings, sleep, relax and eat plenty of Swiss chocolate.

On the dreaded Thursday I team up with a group of ladies who are exploring a nearby village. I try not to clock-watch as midday approaches and succeed so well that it's only later I realise that being on the Continent there is a time lag.

When we get back to the hotel I go to see one of the leaders. He wants to know if I will talk about endurance during the evening meeting. I am with a Christian group and we have a time of fellowship every evening. We go home tomorrow, so tonight's meeting will be the last. I wonder if he knows what he could be letting himself in for once I start talking. So far only the leaders and a nurse know my situation. The nurse had actually been to our house with a youth group a few years before, and when I got on to the usual topic the previous night she ended up in tears as well. I only hope they have a good supply of tissues for this evening's session.

I don't do a great deal of public speaking and I am sure a lot of them will be wondering what a twenty-two-year-old can tell them about endurance, so I start off by explaining that over the last year I have learned an awful lot about it. In the beginning, after the rape, I didn't know how I was going to carry on or what the next day would bring. I just had to take each day at a time and trust that God would be in control. The fact that I am standing in front of them, a bit croaky but otherwise intact, exactly a year to the day, is all the evidence I need of how God has pulled me through. I don't intend playing for sympathy, but by the time I have finished speaking my nurse friend is not the only one in tears.

Two weeks after I return from holiday Pug has her special day. My new relationship is flourishing but somehow I cannot settle. When I hear yet another report about the judge involved in the 'Ealing Vicarage rape case' it is the last straw. I am trying to get my life back together again and all I keep getting are these constant reminders. I ask for a transfer to a branch of Sainsbury's right away from London and pack my bags.

Before I leave, my GP fills in the form for me to claim Criminal Injuries. She has to write a report on my physical and mental state. When I tell her how I felt at various stages over the year she is cross. She wants to know why I didn't tell her before. I did try, but she wasn't there. Nor were my police. I howled my eyes out in the park instead. Perhaps things will be easier in a new area, away from the place where it all happened.

Pug and I leave home just in time. Within a few months of our departure the Vicarage is burgled twice more. Mum jokes that it's no use trying to protect her belongings any more. The intruders only do more damage that way. She will leave everything in as prominent a place as possible, with a note in case they can't find things. In reality it is far from a joke. The police advise on security and a burglar alarm is fitted. All we have to do now is remember the code to get into our own home and cope with a second batch of letters from prisoners. Most of them have committed minor crimes and are protesting about the injustice of their sentences compared to the ones the men in our case received. They have a point, but I don't really want to know. I thought the trial would see an end to it all. Instead it looks like going on for ever.

A Christian magazine for teenagers prints an article about rape, including my experience. One of the national papers takes it up and reinterprets it, so we are involved in yet another legal action. The Radox advertisements don't do a great deal for me either. The smell of stale smoke is utterly revolting. I never really liked it much; now it just says *Them*. I have to get away from it as quickly as possible.

I've heard of instances where people want to scrape all their skin off, to get the men who raped them totally out of their systems. I don't think I've ever felt like that. Our bodies shed their skin every so often anyway, and we are always changing in who we are. I have just clung to that song 'Bread of Life'. I knew I was going to be a new person. God had promised.

Coming to terms with bleeding, of whatever kind, is not quite so straightforward. Anal bleeding particularly. My new GP reckons that cauterising the vein could do more harm than good, so it looks like being one more little thing I have to learn to live with. Like the continuing tests for infections. I thought I'd finished with them until about a month after the court case, Carol told me there was one final test. I never even thought to ask what it was for. I just went along, had the blood test, and as usual rang a week later for the results. I didn't begin to worry until the doctor told me she couldn't give them to me over the phone. She'd always told me before, why the new hesitancy? She explained that if the test was positive I might contemplate throwing myself off Tower Bridge and she wanted me there in front of her to talk it through.

This test was obviously not run-of-the-mill. Nobody mentioned AIDS, but my mind began to work overtime. It was still early days on the AIDS scene and there were all kinds of scare stories going around. A drop of blood could give you AIDS, or someone's saliva, or kissing a person with the infection. If one of the men had it, I wouldn't stand a chance. I remember thinking flippantly that if I was going to fling myself off a bridge I didn't need to go all the way across London to the Tower. There were a lot closer than that. I worked in Chiswick. There was one just down the road.

Due to my persistence I eventually discovered the test was negative, but the thought of it still bugs me. I know so little about the subject. Which test? Was it for HIV or full-blown AIDS? I have heard rumours about how long the disease can lie dormant. Perhaps it wouldn't show up yet? At first I was stunned. Now I am frightened. Who can I ask about it? What questions do I need to put to them? I have moved to a new area, new church, new job. The Sainsbury's job was a bit of a letdown after my last one, and I am now working for a Christian organisation. Few people know my situation. I can't go round introducing myself as the girl from the Ealing Vicarage case, or ask total strangers if they think I have AIDS. Even the people who have known and supported me over the past year and a half only know part of the story. I daren't let on all my anxieties for fear of driving them away. They have their own jobs, their own lives. I know there is a danger of depending on people far more than is healthy. I must not become a leech.

The trouble is that when no one knows the situation, it is all too easy for people to put their foot in it without realising. The December anniversary is still significant. I try not to think of little children and babies, but it's a time mixed with sadness and relief. Everywhere I look there seem to be one-year-olds. It hurts. I might appear to be fine, but inside I am crying like a waterfall. At work one of the women is going through a difficult pregnancy and it looks as though she might miscarry. Someone from another office prays about it in words I will never forget:

'Thank you, Lord, that you never let a child into this world you don't want.'

How I hold back the tears I shall never know. It's like salt being poured into an open wound.

The GP in London recommended that I have a year off work to get over everything. I have had four months off, and several more occasions when I have suffered total exhaustion. The new GP decides that I can not carry on having a couple of weeks off every six months or so. He thinks I should talk to someone rather than trying to sleep through the pain. He suggests the community nurse. What he omits to tell me is that she is the community psychiatric nurse. I do not find out until it is too late to back out. I am less hesitant about telling her my reservations about psychiatry. Despite my opinions we get on well together and I agree to see her on a regular basis. The bonus lies in the fact that I get time for extra sleep after each appointment. They can say what they like about blanking out the hurt. I think I am just plain tired. Nobody seems to appreciate just how exhausting all this talking can be.

CHAPTER
TWENTY-TWO

For the next nine months I find myself looking forward to my visits to the psychiatric nurse. She is very down-to-earth and is prepared to deal with the questions that are worrying me rather than the ones she thinks ought to be causing me problems. I still haven't got over the shock of finding the whole world now knows all about 6 March. I found buggery horrendous. It makes me want to heave when people use it as a swear word or treat it as a joke. Yet the more I have tried to repress or ignore my feelings, the more problems and hang-ups they have been causing.

The nurse helps me to face my reactions and not be afraid of them. She doesn't give me easy options, but points out the opposite extremes and helps me find a point midway, one that I can learn to live with and accept. The relief is enormous. Things are coming back under my control. A similar philosophy applies to big, middle-aged men. I don't have to like everyone in the world. I will wear myself out trying. I have a choice: I can worry about these things for ever, or accept that the memories will take time to heal. I don't have to have everything sorted here and now. It is part of a long-term process.

If I am worried about AIDS I have an option there, too. Helplines are now functioning. I have only to pick up the phone and put myself out of my misery. It sounds fine in theory, but it takes me a year to get round to doing it. Just as I decide to go for it, all the adverts with the telephone number seem to vanish. When one does finally come back on the screen I am sitting in a friend's house, and can hardly sit there scribbling in full view. I have to print the number on my memory and wind myself up later to make a call.

The man at the other end of the line informs me I would not have been tested for AIDS but for HIV. I think his rebuke is a bit much but presume it is a way of making the public less ignorant, and he does tell me what I need to know. The incubation period is three months, although the disease may remain dormant for years. If I have not had intercourse with anyone else I can stop worrying. I feel so stupid when I think of all those months I have tortured myself every time I have had a cold or felt slightly under-the-weather.

One thing still concerns me. What of those who don't receive such good news? I haven't heard of a case where somebody has contacted AIDS from being raped, but it cannot be far off. I have experienced enough prejudice to appreciate what they will have to go through. One day at Sainsbury's people were joking about something and I just said, 'Don't worry. I've had the test', without explaining any further. They gave me such a look. They had no idea how to react.

The rape has changed my whole outlook on life. Suddenly something happened that affected everything I did, what I talked about, the way I lived, the questions I had to face. At twenty-one I was having to consider problems like pregnancy, abortion and adoption. It has made me stronger. I've had to work out problems from the past that were still painful. I'm not saying I've arrived, but I've had to recognise them and come to terms with issues that I wouldn't have had to think about otherwise.

Staring death in the face changed my attitude more than anything. I don't think I realised how close it was at first. I was just praying, 'God, get me out of here alive,' and treating it rather flippantly. It only sank in afterwards how serious it might have been. It has certainly taught me to worry less and enjoy what I've got. When things go wrong I now know it's not a major disaster. The world isn't going to come to an end when I make a mistake. I just have to accept it and carry on.

Life has become so much more important. At the end of the day, possessions, however nice, are not the things of real value. I still have some of my furry animals and about sixty pigs in different shapes and sizes, but I don't put all my hopes on possessions. My animals from the Scrubs are still important, though. Scrubby lost some of his significance when David bled on his ear, but Monkey is very special and Hippo would have been, had he ever come. Even so, they're not quite the same as before. Material things don't stay precious for ever. Feelings move on.

I no longer blame Dad and David for not living up to my ideal of men. In some ways I still see men as the leaders, the protectors, but I've come to realise that there are instances when I have more endurance and stamina than some men. Most of the men I know are weaker than me in many ways. Not physically maybe. It doesn't take much to flatten me, and I will still run from pain. I'm talking about the strength a person has in themselves.

It's taken me a long while to appreciate how difficult it is for men to find themselves victims, especially in a rape situation. Dad seemed to age overnight. His memory has never been the same since, whereas he was spot on before. He says he's handled it emotionally, and I've certainly never seen him upset in any way. Sometimes it seems to hit him, but not for long. He never really expresses much feeling. Either he has handled it and it really doesn't affect him, or he's suppressed it and one day it will catch up with him.

I haven't seen David since our brief meeting at the Old Bailey, but I sometimes wonder how he is faring and if his hearing is any better. He was a very important part of my life. It would have been much more difficult to have got through those first few months without him. I wish there had been someone he could have talked to, people who could have given him more support. He was left with so many things to feel bitter about, and I know the effect bitterness can have. How it can eat away from inside.

I worry about Pug too at times. When I was making her up one day she told me not to put anything round her neck, because she can't bear to feel as if she's being tied up or strangled. I know I should talk more with her, but as I've never felt like that I don't understand it. She's never really got all the things that bothered her out of her system, even though she's had more than a hundred hours of counselling. She had nightmares about what happened at the Vicarage for ages afterwards. In the end I showed her my statement. I'd tried to protect her, but she needed to be part of it. She didn't know where she stood when everything revolved around me instead of both of us. Mum and Dad tried to make it up to her by concentrating on the wedding. Even the psychiatrists saw that as the one good thing we could all share. They may have been mistaken. We all made so much of it that her doubts although expressed then, are only now becoming obvious.

It was so difficult to disentangle prewedding nerves from genuine causes for concern. I often used to worry whether I could cope with married life after the rape. Thankfully my anxieties have proved groundless. The 'good' that it was so important for me to experience has taken away my fears. Sex in a loving relationship is very different to the assault on my person that caused me to switch off emotionally.

We were a bit concerned that details of my wedding arrangements might leak out if the papers got hold of them. Someone did spill the beans about our engagement, but not until several months after the event. We made sure we were as far away from publicity as possible when we got engaged – on the remote edge of Wales where, eight months before, the person I was promising to marry came scrambling down the cliffs to my rescue.

He might not have known what he was letting himself in for

then, but I made sure he was left in no doubt fairly soon afterwards. He can't put the clock back and share my pain, but he knows how much I need to get it out of my system at times. I've been so impressed by his reaction. There seems to be such a deep maturity, an unconditional love. He provides the 'oomph' for me to be strong, and if I don't feel like being strong I don't have to be. He is there.

I might have raised a few eyebrows at my wedding by wearing white, but I felt that if anyone had any questions they could say them to my face. Carol more than anyone helped me over that hurdle. She insisted I should still consider myself a virgin, and once I'd worked that through I was determined to get married in white. The men had taken enough already. They weren't going to take that away from me. Some of the guests didn't know I had a twin and when they saw Pug in green they were a bit confused. They survived though.

Being away from Ealing has helped. I don't usually feel half so nervous when I am alone, unless I watch *Crimewatch* late at night. We live in a terraced house and when they did an item about someone who was going around attacking people in terraced houses it didn't make me feel too wonderful. At first I thought the worst had already happened, so I didn't care what I did. I had to relearn to be cautious. The tube probably bothers me most now, when I go back to London. If I see anybody a bit shifty I am on my guard straightaway. I won't get in the carriage with them, or I watch to make sure they aren't following me off the train.

Anniversaries are hard too. I was actually flying back across the Channel when the *Herald of Free Enterprise* sank on 6 March 1987. The following year it was 'Death on the Rock', three IRA people killed in Gibraltar. There always seems to be some tragedy to hit headline news and stay in the paper for days around that time. My body grows so tense beforehand that it invariably starts the bleeding again. When it doesn't, that will be another major achievement.

CHAPTER
TWENTY-THREE

It's only recently that I've begun to realise that it was not just Dad and Pug and Dave, the people closest to me, who were affected by the rape. It must have been particularly hard for them because they were trying to help me and come to terms with their feelings at the same time, but others were fighting their own battles too, a fact that often got forgotten when we became preoccupied with our traumas. One of my friends was on the verge of a nervous breakdown when the rape happened, and that was the final straw as far as she was concerned. She told me straight out one day: 'You pushed me over the edge.' I felt flattered to think she cared so much, but it just pointed out how little we take other people's feelings into account. I'm amazed that people still need to talk about it and to know that I'm not afraid to confront their worries and anxieties. We just slog it out and hope at the end we all have a better understanding. Then, when they hear other people with distorted views, hopefully they will be able to correct some of them.

Talking has been so important, from that first crude conversation with Jim that helped to exorcise some of the ghosts in my room, through to a recent one with two girls who were staying with us. They couldn't believe that I still had the beanbag that was in my bedroom, or the duvet cover and towel. The only thing I haven't got is the sheet, even though it was almost brand-new. Much to my annoyance, Mum made me throw it out when it came back from the police. I was determined not to be beaten. There have been so many things that could throw me – if I let them. I've found out since that my mother's family motto is 'Win through'. It seems very appropriate.

I am no longer able to go to the carol service at Wormwood Scrubs, although I have been to one more play there. Knowing something of conditions in prison I fear for the men at times. So many awful things can happen. Homosexual rape. Attacks on people's lives. I know it has not been easy for them, and I can't see the outside world being much of a picnic for them when they are released. All I can do is go on praying that they will be healed, not just physically, but from all the things in the past that have led them to act the way they did.

I had a dream back in the summer that I was asked to help with the rehabilitation of one of them. My first reaction was 'No, I couldn't handle it', but when I was thinking about it afterwards I realised that they could repent and turn round. They have shown some remorse. It is possible that they may see another way to the life they have been living. As far as forgiveness is concerned, I am not prepared to condemn them any more than is necessary. They are three men who committed a crime and are paying for it in prison. If they don't choose to accept my forgiveness that is their problem. Just as they are the ones who have to live with the consequences of their choice if they reject God.

In some ways I have found it harder to forgive the judge. He was a highly respected man who had been empowered to give judgements on behalf of the nation, but it didn't sound as though he had the nation's support when he implied that because we could forgive the men they didn't need such a severe punishment. Our reactions didn't alter the crime. In legal terms justice still needed to be done. Otherwise Christians would never get justice in a British court.

There are many people who want to know why there was such a big outcry over our case. Every day there are reports of rapists being jailed for only two or three years. The question shouldn't be why the sentencing in the Ealing Vicarage rape case caused so much controversy, but why any rapist should get away with a light sentence. There doesn't seem to be sufficient understanding of how damaging rape is. It should be taken much more seriously. Victims should not be treated as though they are the guilty party. Judges should talk to rape victims and hear first-hand about the trauma involved. I made the mistake of not telling people how badly I was being affected. None of the medical staff really knew until afterwards, especially about my feeling suicidal.

It's hardly surprising that women are often reluctant to report rape. I know the choice has to be theirs, and theirs alone, but I would still urge other victims to go to the police and report the attack. If men think they can get away with it what is there to stop them ruining someone else's life? Not all police may be as understanding and supportive as mine were, but they are working on improving their approach to victims of sexual crimes and the new rape suites are a definite move in the right direction.

Things are changing slowly, partly as a result of our case. A lot of work has been put into securing total anonymity for the victims of rape. A bill was presented to the House of Commons by Harry Greenway on 2 February 1987, the day our case went to court. It became law that summer. Two years later I was listening to the radio when I heard that the law of appeal is also changing. In future victims in certain cases will be able to appeal against low sentencing. I shouted at the radio 'Two years too late.' It could have made such a difference if we had been able to go to the Appeal Court. The compensation I received from Criminal Injuries showed that not everyone believed the trauma I had suffered was not so great. Forgiving does not necessarily mean forgetting. There is no rule that says a person is going to recover from rape just like that. I don't suppose I will ever be able to forget entirely, but the smaller details that somehow made things worse are going. Time does help to heal memories if they are faced and accepted. I have come across many people who are not able to forgive because they are relying on their own strength. They are often the ones who end up addicted to tranquillisers or alcohol, afraid to go out, or unable to maintain relationships with the opposite sex. I'm not saying I don't have problems, but I have the greatest forgiver there has ever been on my side. I don't have to go it alone. Neither does any woman. No one needs to end up like the lady who had carried the burden for sixty odd years.

I had another letter from someone in a similar situation to hers recently. My advice to her, or any woman, is simply TALK, TALK, TALK. There has to be someone, somewhere, who will listen, or who can point you in the right direction for help. People are gradually becoming more aware and there are organisations set up specifically to give support. To say nothing of the help family and friends may give – if we will let them.

Rape does not have to mean the end of everything, however horrific it has been. I have learned since that the things I had so much difficulty coming to terms with were not unique to my experience. It makes me wonder where rapists get their ideas in the first place, the kind of influence porn must be having. They just can't think these things up out of thin air. Seeing the effects drugs and alcohol can have has made me very wary too. It's not just the damage that is done to the individual but to the people who come into contact with that person when they are not fully in control of their actions. They have to live with the consequences as well, sometimes for the rest of their lives.

The trauma associated with rape is very great. Anyone who does not believe that should try living through it. There are definite stages, though nobody really explained that to me at first. That's one of the reasons I want to share my experience. So nobody need feel she is cracking up, or going mad, when she is sitting there feeling the greyness, the nothingness. If someone else has gone through similar feelings there can be some form of reassurance that it is all part of a normal pattern, however abnormal it feels.

I still don't know how some women get over it if they don't have the kind of support I have received. God provided me with some very special friends who kept very close to me. Even so, it was touch and go at times. Women need to be able to talk about their experience to get it out of their system. Trying to ignore the fact that it's happened can create far more problems. Carol was right. You can bury it dead, or you can bury it alive. Talking with someone who is prepared to listen and to make some attempt to understand is one of the most effective ways of burying it dead. I know; I've done enough of it over the months and years since the rape. It doesn't take long to sort out who can handle it, and who will go to pieces at the very thought. The hardest part is getting to the point of acknowledging your needs, and being prepared to ask for help. So many people have difficulty initiating a conversaton. I don't suffer from that problem. I jump in first so no one need worry about treading on my toes.

I sometimes wonder if people are thinking 'Here she goes again', but if they actually listen and take note they would see there is a lot behind what I am saying. I'm not just speaking on my own behalf, but for all those women who haven't been able to express their feelings. Talking about the subject wears me out but it's worth it if other people find their own understanding increased. Quite often someone will come up to me afterwards and share how they have been attacked or abused. Maybe years earlier. So many women haven't been able to talk about it. They're afraid. Or they feel guilty in some way.

There are times when I wish I could leave it behind. I had a real battle with God at a conference last year. I felt He was telling me to talk about my experience and I was arguing 'Can't I forget it? Just this once?' I didn't get any peace till I opened my mouth and told everyone I'd been raped. They didn't work out the circumstances for a long while afterwards, then it took over a year before one of the women told me that my story had helped her to face up to the fact that she had been raped years before. At last she had been able to seek counselling for it.

I was on the point of talking with rape victims referred to me by Carol, but I left London before that became a possibility. My furry animals are doing a good job, though. Every so often I collect up an armful and give them to a friend who works with abused children. She is able to give them to the children with the promise that they have come from someone who knows what they have been through, and has come out the other side.

Life does go on. Not always wonderfully, but it is possible to win through. I discovered there was a lot in life I could enjoy once I chose to live on, rather than just exist. It doesn't mean I never hit rough times, but it is possible to face them. Head on. Because life was horrendous once it doesn't mean an easy ride for the rest of the journey; there's always the good and the bad. There are no easy solutions; people have got to work at it. Be persistent. Learn to face up to the knocks that will come.

The world is an ugly place. Sometimes I just sit in front of the television and want to howl my eyes out when I hear the news. But these things do happen. It's no use falling to pieces all the time. I cope by praying for specific people, like the children who have my toys. I feel I've got some kind of link with them even if I haven't met them.

All this has taught me in a special way that no one is beyond the scope of God's love. Some may never have known real security with people. Human relationships often fall short of our expectations. Without God I would not be here today. Whenever I get into hassles I can't handle I hand them back to Him and say, 'Right, God. Come on. You've got to take over.' I have had to learn to let Him work on his terms, though, and not try to dictate them. It was only when I stopped trying to fight my own battles and admitted my weakness that I discovered God was there. He was there when I was being attacked and no human person came to my aid. The joy I was able to experience after the rape was so supernatural it just said, 'Look. God is so much greater than you could expect. He'll carry you through the tough times.' He didn't leave me alone to get on with it. Whenever I recognised my need He was in there with me, pouring out his love through others to me.

I have discovered that love is gentle, patient, ready to put itself in the other person's position and share the anger and the hurt. It does not expect the person to 'snap out of it' and recover overnight, or even after several years. Anyone recovering from the effects of rape needs a great deal of love. Rape is totally and utterly destructive, striking right at the roots of a person's sense of self and worth. I would not have believed that the events of one hour on 6 March 1986 could have such devastating effects. I can only thank God for all those who have helped in the healing, male and female. However unlikely it might once have seemed, this rape has most definitely been a love story.

John, John, Steve, Mickey, Carol, Julie, Julie, Liz, Elizabeth, Shirley, James, Chuck, Alan, Roy, David, David, Ian, Rita, Gary, Warren, Wendy, Debbie, Chris, Chris, Catherine, David, Steve, Andy, Tim, Nigel, Jeanette, Sarah, Jane, Roger, Gladys, Elsie, Lilly, Molly, Marjorie, Jerry, Marion, Graeme, John, Jean, Keith, Annie, Roy, the Kerrs, Jack, Dylan, Aled, Alwyn, Rodney, Gareth, Colin, Lucy, Tracey, Pru, Clare, Trudy, Margaret, Jean, John, Paul, Lisa, the actors of D wing – Wormwood Scrubs, Fish, Marillion, Andy, Chris, and my family.

Thank you all.